TENNESSEE
LEGENDS AND LORE

TENNESSEE
LEGENDS AND LORE

ALAN BROWN

Published by The History Press
Charleston, SC
www.historypress.com

First published 2023

Manufactured in the United States

ISBN 9781467153362

Library of Congress Control Number: 2022947094

CONTENTS

INTRODUCTION

The state of Tennessee takes its name from the Cherokee village of Tanasi. One could say that Tennessee is not a typical southern state, even though it did join the Confederacy during the Civil War. It earned the nickname "The Volunteer State" during the War of 1812, when 3,500 Tennesseans enlisted in the army. However, during the Civil War, Tennessee's participation was less enthusiastic, with eastern Tennessee favoring remaining a part of the Union. In fact, Tennessee provided more Union soldiers than any other state in the Confederacy. Slavery was prevalent in West Tennessee, where large plantations grew cotton, tobacco and corn. However, because eastern Tennessee's mountainous geography was not ideally suited to agriculture, slavery was rare in those counties. Consequently, with slaves comprising only 25 percent of the state's total population, Tennessee had the smallest slave population of all the states in the Confederacy. Tennessee was the last state to join the Confederacy, due mostly to the state's political divisions. More battles were fought in Tennessee than in any other state, with the exception of Virginia, because of the state's central location. At the end of the war, Tennessee was the first state to be readmitted to the Union.

Tennessee is unique in other ways as well. Although country music is popular throughout the entire South, the unofficial capital of country music is in Nashville, Tennessee. A number of Tennesseans have become national heroes, such as frontiersman Davy Crockett, who died defending the Alamo; Sergeant Alvin York, winner of the Congressional Medal of Honor in

World War I; and Dr. Martin Luther King Jr., who was assassinated by James Earl Ray while showing his support for sanitation workers in Memphis. In one of the most important trials in United States history, Dayton high school teacher John Thomas Scopes was tried and found guilty of violating Tennessee's Butler Act, which prohibited the teaching of evolution. During World War II, the federal government produced weapons-grade enriched uranium at Oakridge, a special community created to house the workers.

However, Tennessee also stands out because of its folklore. In this book, *Tennessee Legends and Lore*, the reader will learn about the ghosts of the Civil War, such as the phantom sentry who is still keeping track of the movements of enemy forces from his perch on top of Lookout Mountain. The exploits of the land pirate John Murrel have entered the realm of legend because they are almost too horrible to believe. One of the spine-tingling legends in this book is the story of little Nina Craigmiles, whose mausoleum is said to "weep blood" because the child died so young. Another legend of a child ghost is the tale of a twelve-year-old girl named Mary, who was struck and killed by a car in front of the Orpheum Theatre in the early 1920s. Even famous actors like Yul Brynner have seen her apparition sitting in seat C5 in the auditorium. New England might be famous for its witch trials, but Tennessee has probably the most infamous witch in the entire country, Kate Batts, whose feats astounded even Andrew Jackson. A number of monsters lurk in the pages of *Tennessee Legends and Lore*, including a Bigfoot-like creature known as the Flintville Monster. Creatures from Native American folklore, like Reelfoot, Spearfinger and the Wampus Cat, appear in this book as well.

So if you are looking for a sometimes unnerving but always fascinating supplement to Tennessee's historical record, you can find it in *Tennessee Legends and Lore*. You will never think of the Volunteer State the same way again.

Chapter 1

CIVIL WAR LEGENDS

The Battle of Fort Donelson

Dover

After the fall of Fort Henry to the Union army in February 1862, Confederate reinforcements were quickly dispatched to Fort Donelson, ten miles away, to prevent it from surrendering as well. On February 13, Brigadier General John McClernand attempted, unsuccessfully, to take a Confederate battery. General Ulysses Simpson Grant's forces tried bombarding Fort Donelson with shells from the east. On February 15, following a strong push by the Confederate army, Confederate general Gideon Pillow ordered his men back to the entrenchments instead of escaping. Consequently, General Grant counterattacked and completely surrounded the Confederates, forcing them to surrender the fort on February 16. Only a few thousand Confederates fled to safety. This was the first major Union victory of the entire war and a major defeat for the Confederates, who lost control of Kentucky as a result.

Many visitors to Fort Donelson report hearing the residual sounds of battle. Gunshots and cannon fire are the most commonly heard spectral noises at the fort. Others have heard the rhythmic plodding of phantom armies as they march across the battlefield. The distinctive rebel yell occasionally resounds over the battlefield, leading some to believe that the ghosts of Confederate soldiers are cheering the sinking of Union gunboats by Confederate cannons.

General Grant's takeover of Fort Donelson was the first major Union victory of the Civil War. *Wikimedia Commons.*

In many cases, the carnage left by the Civil War has found its way into private homes and businesses. Such is the case with the Dover Hotel. It was built between 1851 and 1853 as a "home away from home" for riverboat travelers. Confederate general Simon B. Buckner commandeered the hotel as his headquarters during the Battle of Fort Donelson. After the battle, it served as a field hospital. The Dover Hotel is also known as the Surrender House because this is where General Buckner accepted General Grant's terms of surrender. After the historic hotel was converted into a museum, a volunteer was closing up for the day when the full-bodied apparition of a Union soldier materialized right in front of her for a few seconds before vanishing.

Civil War reenactors have proven to be very good sources of battlefield ghost stories. In his blog *The Late Unpleasantness*, author Christopher Coleman writes about the experiences of Civil War reenactors at Fort Donelson. One of them said that while he was on picket duty, he saw the glowing head and torso of an officer with a broad-brimmed hat headed toward him. The fact that the apparition was smoking a cigar led the sentry to believe that he had just seen the ghost of General Ulysses S. Grant—or part of him, at least. A female reenactor who was playing the role of a sutler said that she was awakened in her tent one night by the clanging sound of her wares vibrating violently. No strong winds were blowing through the camp that night. The past reasserts itself unexpectedly at Fort Donelson.

The Battle of Franklin

Franklin

The ultimate goal of Confederate general John Hood's Tennessee campaign was to prevent Union general William Tecumseh Sherman's army from burning Savannah, Georgia. After passing through Alabama and Georgia in 1864, Hood moved into Tennessee with the intention of preventing Major General John M. Schofield's Fourth Corps from joining up with the rest of the Army of the Cumberland in Nashville. On November 24, Hood attempted to intercept Schofield's army at the Duck River crossing. When that plan failed, Hood tried again to engage the Fourth Corps at Spring Hill. Following a series of skirmishes between the two armies, Hood decided to cease fighting and retire for the night. Unknown to Hood, Schofield's men had sneaked out of Spring Hill during the night and were headed twelve miles north to the town of Franklin.

On November 30, Union general Jacob D. Cox arrived at Franklin before Schofield. Cox set up his command post at Franklin Carter's house on the west side of the Columbia Pike. When Schofield arrived, he deployed two divisions to hold a bridge south of Franklin. Meanwhile, Hood set up his defenses on the south end of town. Late in the afternoon, Hood committed a grave error by ordering a frontal assault on Schofield's Fourth Corps, despite protests from his officers that the Union forces were too strong. The battlefield, which was two miles long and one and a half miles wide, was the scene of horrific fighting. Men fought with anything available, at times using their rifle butts as clubs. Much of the bloodiest fighting took place around the Carter house. By nightfall, nine thousand men lay dead or dying. Two-thirds of the casualties were Confederate. The five-hour battle proved be one of the bloodiest in the entire war. Six Confederate generals were killed in the melee. Hundreds of Confederate were treated at Carnton Mansion, which was converted into a field hospital. The Federals escaped to Nashville, leaving the Confederate army in shambles behind them.

Many of the houses in Franklin were impacted by the battle raging around them. One of these homes was Carnton Mansion. Using slave labor, a politician named Randal McGavock built the house in 1826 on a limestone foundation. On the front porch of the two-story, twenty-two-room brick mansion are seven resplendent white columns. Many of the furnishings in the interior are original. The woodwork is faux rosewood and mahogany. The beauty of this antebellum mansion belies the bloody role it played during the Battle of Franklin.

At the time of the Civil War, Randal McGavock's son, John, and his wife, Caroline, were living in Carnton Mansion. On November 30, 1864, the McGavock family's life was changed forever. In the first night following the battle, over three hundred wounded and dying soldiers were brought to the mansion, which was converted into a field hospital. Servants rolled up the carpets, and Mrs. McGavock tore up clothing for bandages. Bloodstains on the floor speak to the agony endured by the men who were treated there, especially in a southern-facing bedroom where surgeries were performed. Approximately half of the soldiers who were brought there succumbed to their injuries, despite the best efforts of the doctors. According to legend, the pile of corpses behind the mansion formed a sort of column. The bodies of four Confederate generals who had died of their wounds lay in state on the back porch, where their men could salute them for one last time.

Two days later, the bodies of approximately 1,700 soldiers who were killed in battle were hastily buried near the mansion. Moved by the sacrifices made by these soldiers, John McGavock had their bodies exhumed and moved to a permanent resting place on the grounds of Carnton. The City of Franklin covered the cost of burial: five dollars per body. The descendants of John and Caroline McGavock tended the burial plot until Susie Lee McGavock sold the plantation in 1911.

This site of so much suffering and death is said to be very haunted. One of the spirits is the ghost of a little girl who died in the house in 1840. She tends to make her presence known by breaking glass. The pensive ghost of a Confederate general has been sighted pacing back and forth on the back porch. This apparition has also been seen walking around the backyard. The ghost of the cook who served the McGavock family and married a field slave remains in the mansion. She has been seen floating through the kitchen where she worked for so many years. Tour guides have also heard the sounds of an invisible presence in the kitchen, preparing meals and cleaning up. Her disembodied head is clearly visible in photographs taken in the hallway. The sounds of heavy footsteps by a spirit wearing boots have been heard

Used as a field hospital during the Battle of Franklin, Carnton Mansion is said to be haunted by a number of ghosts, including the spirits of a little girl, a cook and several Native Americans. *Alan Brown.*

as well. Other spirits are believed to have made the mansion their eternal home, including a girl with long, brown hair, a lady in white and Native Americans who lived on the property long before Randal McGavock built his lovely mansion there.

Built in 1830 by Fountain Branch Carter, the Carter House was located in the very heart of the battle. After the Federals arrived in Franklin, General Jacob Cox informed the Carter family that he was taking over their home as his headquarters. As the battle commenced the next day, Fountain Branch Carter's son, Lieutenant Colonel Moscow Branch Carter, ushered the family downstairs to the cellar for safety. All told, Fountain Branch Carter; three of his daughters, Lieutenant Colonel Carter's sisters; Fountain Branch Carter's daughter-in-law; a few children; and several neighbors and slaves huddled in the cellar while the battle raged around them. Their battlefield experience consisted mostly of sound as bullets hit the outside of the house and wounded and dying men screamed in agony. They also heard the sounds of hand-to-hand combat inside the house and out on the porch. The end must have seemed near indeed when a cannonball struck the side of the house. The

Visitors and staff have seen the ghosts of Todd and Annie Carter inside the Carter House. *Alan Brown.*

Confederates made repeated attempts to breach the Union headquarters but with no success.

Late that night, after the fighting died down, the Carter family learned that Moscow's brother, Todd Carter, was one of the thousands of wounded and dying soldiers who lay in the field around the house. With lantern in hand, Moscow ventured out into the darkness, accompanied by General Thomas Benton Smith, Todd's commanding officer, and several other soldiers who had served with Todd. The searchers found the young man only one hundred yards away from the house. They carried him into the house and laid him in a bedroom on the first floor. Todd died two days later.

The Carter House has been open to the public since 1953. A number of strange occurrences have taken place inside the house during tours. Visitors and tour guides have heard disembodied voices. Some people have felt invisible hands tugging on their clothes. On one occasion, a statue inside the house began jumping up and down while a tour guide was chronicling the history of the house. Tour guides feel that this could be the way the ghost of Todd's little sister, Annie, is trying to get attention. The spirit of Todd

Carter is believed to be the ghost that has been seen sitting on the edge of the bed in the room where Todd died. Undoubtedly, the trauma suffered by the bystanders and the participants in the battle has left its psychic imprint on the walls and timbers of the Carter House.

Another house that became ground zero during the Battle of Franklin was the Lotz House. A master woodworker from Germany named Albert Lotz built his four-column Greek Revival house in 1858 on five acres purchased from the Carter family. By the time the Union army arrived in Franklin from Spring Hill, Albert Lotz was living in the frame house along with his wife, Margaretha, and their six children. When the Federals began digging trenches south of the Lotz House on November 30, Lotz grabbed his woodworking tools and ushered his family into the Carter House, which was safer because it was built of brick. While Lotz and his family sat on the floor of the Carter family's cellar, a cannonball smashed through a wall and landed on the first floor.

When the sounds of battle finally died down, the Carter and Lotz families emerged from their underground shelter. In his diary, Albert Lotz wrote that the bodies of fallen soldiers were piled six feet deep between his house and the

So many corpses were piled up in front of the Lotz House during the Battle of Franklin that they appeared to be standing up. *Alan Brown.*

Carter House. Lotz added that there were so many bodies in his front yard that some of the dead soldiers appeared to be standing up, like scarecrows. When the Lotz family returned to their home, they found that cannon fire had made large holes in the roof and floors. Despite the damage inflicted on the house, it was used as a field hospital for both Confederate and Union soldiers. Albert and Margaretha were forced to move to San Jose, California, following the public outcry over a piano he had made with an offensive carving on the lid portraying an American eagle with an American flag in one claw and a Confederate flag facing downward in the other claw. Over the next century, the Lotz House housed a variety of businesses, including a sandwich shop, an attorney's office, a bakery, a cooking school, a flower shop and a gift shop. The Lotz House was listed in the National Register of Historic Places in 1976. In 2001, J.T. Thompson purchased the Lotz House and converted it into a museum, which opened seven years later.

Over the years, people who have lived and worked in the Lotz House have reported a variety of uncanny occurrences. In fact, in 2010, the Travel Channel proclaimed the Lotz House to be the "second most terrifying place in America." Tour guides claim that exhibits and artifacts, such as bottles and pipes, have been moved to different spots in the house during the night. Spectral drumming occasionally disturbs the silence of the house at night. Passersby have seen ghostly figures staring out of the windows after the house has closed. Spectral Confederate soldiers make "unscheduled appearances" in various rooms in the house. Unseen hands have pulled on the pants legs of visitors. According to Margie Thessin, the owner of Franklin on Foot Walking Tours, a visitor gazed down a hallway and saw the apparition of a woman holding a candle. The visitor clearly remembered hearing the spirit saying, "Where is Ann?" In an interview with WSMV television in 2014, J.T. Thompson said, "When you consider what happens inside the house and on the property surrounding the house, I can't imagine anything more terrifying."

THE BATTLE OF LOOKOUT MOUNTAIN

Chattanooga

After the Battle of Chickamauga, Confederate general Braxton Bragg positioned the Army of Tennessee on Lookout Mountain and Missionary Ridge in an effort to starve the Union army in Chattanooga into

Lookout Mountain has been the site of Revolutionary War battles, Civil War battles and clashes between settlers and Native Americans. *Alan Brown.*

surrendering. Under the command of General Ulysses S. Grant, Union forces captured Brown's Ferry. As a result, much-needed supplies could be transported to his men. On November 24, General Joseph Hooker's 12,000 Union troops began making their way up Lookout Mountain under a cloak of fog. By the time the 1,200 Confederate defenders were able to see the advancing Yankees, it was too late. By late afternoon, Bragg's men had begun abandoning their posts on the mountain. On November 25, Union forces drove the Confederates off Missionary Ridge, thereby breaking the Confederate stranglehold on Chattanooga.

In his book *Ghosts of Lookout Mountain*, author Larry Hillhouse includes a story about one of the sentries who used Lookout Mountain's scenic overlooks to keep watch over the mountain trails along which both the Union and Confederate armies transported supplies. One of these observation points was a nearly invisible spot on a major supply route used by the Union army. Using a lantern, Confederate sentries were able to flash signals to their comrades without risking detection by the enemy. On days when Union soldiers were nowhere in sight, sentries built small fires and communicated with their comrades using smoke signals.

A ghostly sentry is still keeping watch from his post on top of Lookout Mountain. *Alan Brown.*

According to legend, one of these sentries was an injured Confederate soldier who tried to prove his usefulness by keep track of the movements of Union forces along the trail. He was so fearful of being seen by the enemy that he was reluctant to move from his hiding place long enough to find something to eat. Eventually, the duty-bound soldier died of starvation. To this day, people living on or around Lookout Mountain report seeing flashes of light from the mountaintop. Intermittent plumes of smoke have been sighted floating up into the sky. The folkloric explanation for these phenomena is that the ghost of the wounded Confederate sentry is still doing his job, even in the afterlife.

In her book *Ghosts of the Southern Tennessee Valley*, author Georgiana C. Kotarski writes about the experiences of a rock band staying in a house on Shingle Road about one hundred yards down from the Cravens House on Lookout Mountain in the early 1980s. One night, they were rehearsing when they heard a large number of field drums in the distance. After the band members retired for the night, the ghostly drumming grew louder and louder. The next day, one of the band members was in his room, staring at a poster commemorating the Battle of Lookout Mountain. The dates of the battle were listed as November 24–25, the same dates that the men heard the spectral drums.

The Battle of Stones River

Murfreesboro

In late December 1863, the Union general-in-chief, under orders from President Abraham Lincoln, sent a telegraph to General William Rosecrans in Nashville demanding that he drive Confederate general Braxton Bragg's Army of Tennessee out of the state. On December 26, Rosecrans's Army of the Cumberland advanced toward the Confederate defenses in Murfreesboro. Determined to prevent the Union army from advancing any farther toward Chattanooga, Bragg positioned his army on both sides of Stones River at a place where his forces could guard the roads leading to the supply depot in Murfreesboro. Because Bragg did not order his men to dig entrenchments, he advertently exposed them to enemy fire.

On December 31, Bragg ordered his troops to move from left to right on the west side of the river, where they forced Union general M.D. McCook's men to retreat. Eventually, the Federals blocked the Confederate advance. By noon, the fiercest fighting had centered on the Union lines in the Rotund Forest. The Forty-Fourth Mississippi Regiment, armed only with sticks, and Confederate brigadier general Daniel S. Donelson's Tennessee Brigade tried but failed to breach the Union center. When Confederate general Leonidas Polk's reinforcements arrived just before two o'clock in the afternoon, they were cut down by Union gunfire. At four o'clock, Lieutenant General William J. Hardee informed General Bragg that he could not order another assault on Union lines without reinforcements.

An uneasy calm settled over the battlefield until January 2, when Bragg ordered Breckenridge to drive the Federals back across the river. In the face of murderous fire, Breckenridge's troops were forced to retreat after an hour and twenty minutes. After receiving word that reinforcements had joined Rosecrans's army, Bragg initiated the Confederate retreat from Murfreesboro at eleven o'clock at night on January 3 under heavy rainfall. Meanwhile, the Army of the Cumberland set about constructing a fortification as an occupation base. By battle's end, each side had lost around thirteen thousand men.

Not surprisingly, the Stones River Battlefield is a hotbed of ghostly occurrences. A great deal of the paranormal activity is audible. Many visitors and employees have reported hearing the residual sounds of battle, including screams, moans, voices and sporadic gunshots and cannon fire. The rhythmic sound of marching feet occasionally disrupts the stillness of

Many visitors have left the "Slaughter Pen," the most haunted part of Stones River Battlefield, with a "chill bump feeling." *Alan Brown.*

the battlefield. The most memorable of these sounds are the ghostly strains of songs like "Yankee Doodle," "Dixie" and "Home Sweet Home," which the military bands on both sides played at the end of the day.

The most haunted place in the battlefield is undoubtedly the so-called slaughter pen. So many of Union general Phil Sheridan's troops were killed there when the Confederates caught them off guard that the ground was spongy with mud, reminding the farmers among the troops of an actual slaughter pen. The most commonly sighted specter in the slaughter pen is a lone soldier who has been seen sitting on the ground with his legs crossed, as if warming himself by a campfire. He appears to be oblivious to anyone who passes by. Eyewitnesses who were bold enough to engage him in conversation say that he vanished as soon as they started speaking to him.

The best-known spirit on the battlefield is the ghost of Union lieutenant colonel Julius Garesché. Friends of his said that as he was mounting his horse just before the battle commenced, he had a premonition of his own death. Shaken but not deterred from his duty, Colonel Garesché boldly rode into the fray. When he reached the southeast corner of the present-day

Union lieutenant colonel Julius Garesché was decapitated by a cannonball at the southeast corner of present-day Stones River Battlefield near the railroad track. *Alan Brown.*

Stones River Cemetery near the railroad, a cannonball tore off his head. His white horse continuing galloping for twenty yards until Garesché's headless corpse, still seated in the saddle, fell off onto the ground. Colonel Garesché was buried in the Stones River Cemetery.

In their book *Haunted Battlefields of the South*, authors Bryan Bush and Thomas Freese recount the paranormal experiences of visitors at several different sites on the battlefield. Back in the early 2000s, a woman and her son were walking through the battlefield when they were assailed with a barrage of otherworldly sounds. The two had walked just a short way when the son exclaimed, "I hear bees buzzing around my head." The boy's mother, who was sensitive to the presence of spirits, informed him that what he was hearing was actually the whiz of bullets flying through the air. When the boy continued hearing strange sounds, like distant blasts of cannon fire and the neighing of a horse, he had to agree with his mother that Stones River Battlefield was haunted.

In 2002, three Civil War reenactors—two male and one female—were crossing the battlefield, listening to the park's historical audiotapes, when the

A reenactor was filling his canteen at the faucet at the right-hand corner of the visitors' center when he saw the ghost of a Confederate soldier. Also, a park ranger and her dog felt very uncomfortable near the flagpole. *Alan Brown.*

woman stopped walking. Her male companions called out to her, but she was unable to respond. When they caught up to her, she seemed to be out of breath. After a minute or so, she said that she had been overcome with a feeling of intense cold. Then she felt like something had just struck her in the chest. Unable to come up with a rational explanation, the reenactors wondered if she might have inadvertently walked over the spot where a soldier had been shot and killed over a century before.

Many of the full-bodied apparitions sighted on the battlefield are believed to have appeared at the place where they were killed. Some of the ghosts seem to be so lifelike that they have been mistaken for reenactors. In one of these encounters, a park ranger named Jeffrey Leathers was participating in a reenactment when he walked to the visitors' center to refill his canteen. As he rounded a curve in the walkway, Leathers noticed a soldier standing behind a clump of bushes. Assuming that one of the reenactors was pranking him, Leathers ordered the man to come out where he could see him. The soldier raised both of his arms, indicating that he was surrendering. As Leathers raised his gun, the soldier collapsed on the ground and disappeared. When Leathers walked up the place where he assumed the reenactor lay, he could find no trace of the man, not even footprints in the soft mud leading toward the spot.

Another park ranger who had a brush with the uncanny in the battlefield is Laura Stresemann, who worked at the battlefield between 1997 and 2003. In an interview with Dan Whittle, a reporter for the *Cannon Courier*, she said that her pet greyhound, Abby, would shake uncontrollably whenever they approached the flagpole on their daily walks. Stresemann also experienced a ten-degree drop in temperature every time she walked through a part of the battlefield that she called a "cold spot" on sultry summer days. When asked whether or not she believed that there are spirits haunting Stones River Battlefield, Stresemann replied, "I'm sure there are."

Cherry Mansion

Savannah

In 1815, James Rudd built a log cabin near his ferryboat landing on the Tennessee River. The property was located on a prehistoric settlement established two thousand years earlier. In 1830, Rudd sold the land to David Robinson, who tore down the cabin and replaced it with a large house, which he gave to his daughter as a wedding present when she married W.H. Cherry. The house is marked by eighteen-inch-thick walls, handmade bookshelves and cabinets, heart pine flooring and a low stone wall along the perimeter of the house. Robinson went on to make a fortune shipping cotton to Memphis.

During the Civil War, Cherry was a Union sympathizer, as were many of the residents of Savannah. When the Yankees arrived in Savannah in March 1862, Cherry offered his home as the officers' headquarters. General Grant had arrived at Cherry Mansion in March by boat from Fort Henry to prepare his troops for what he hoped would be a decisive battle with the Confederate army. On April 6, Grant was having breakfast with several of his generals when distant cannon fire signaled the Confederates' surprise attack on the Union soldiers at Pittsburg Landing nine miles away. Grant rose from the table and announced, "Gentlemen, the ball is in motion. Let us be off!" Setting down his coffee cup, Grant exited the dining room.

All of Grant's generals joined him in Shiloh, with the exception of General C.L. Smith, who had skinned his shin on the seat of a rowboat in late March. Because the wound had not healed, Smith was confined to his

Two of General Grant's generals died at Cherry Mansion. *Wikimedia Commons.*

bed in Cherry Mansion. Soon, gangrene set in, and Smith died at Cherry Mansion in late April.

Smith was not the only one of Grant's generals who died at Cherry Mansion. In the heat of the battle, General W.H.L. Wallace was defending his position against Confederate artillery at a place that came to be known as "the Hornet's Nest" when he was struck in the head and was taken to Cherry Mansion for medical care. Around the same time, his wife, Martha Ann, had had a premonition that her husband was going to die in battle, so she booked passage on a steamboat bound for Savannah. After she arrived, she took up her position by her husband's bedside. On the fourth day, General Wallace muttered the words, "We shall meet in heaven," and passed away.

Spirits from Cherry Mansion's Civil War past first became really active in 1975. A Civil War demonstrator at the battlefield named Terry Smith who lived close to Cherry Mansion agreed to feed and water the animals and keep an eye on the house while the owners were away. One day, after he had finished his chores at the mansion, he was walking across the yard to his house when he decided to check to see if the front door was locked. Smith was standing in front of the door when he happened to look up at the attic window above the front porch and noticed a bearded man in a blue uniform staring down at him. The man's wide-brimmed hat indicated that he was probably an officer. The stranger's eyes met Smith's, sending shivers down Smith's spine. Smith took off and ran all the way back to his house. While he was catching his breath inside his house, it occurred to him that two Union generals—General Smith and General Wallace—had died inside the house while being treated for their wounds. It was at that moment that he realized he had probably just had an encounter with a ghost from the Civil War.

In June 1976, Terry Smith was sitting on the front porch of Cherry Mansion with the owners' daughter, Mary Ann Guinn, when they noticed a distinguished-looking gray-haired gentleman wearing a white linen suit walking briskly up the drive. When the figure reached the historical marker in front of the house, he vanished. The couple searched the neighborhood but found no trace of the man. Before going home, Terry recalled the experience of a servant in the house. She had told Terry that on several occasions, she heard someone running across the front porch, but no one was ever there. The Guinns did not take the servant seriously; Terry, on the other hand, believed her because of his own sighting at the historic home.

SHILOH NATIONAL BATTLEFIELD

Hardin County

By April 1863, Union forces had taken Kentucky and were advancing up the Tennessee and Cumberland Rivers. After Grant defeated the Confederates at Fort Henny and Fort Donelson in February, Confederate general Albert Sidney Johnston moved his forty-five thousand troops to Corinth, an important rail center. Grant, meanwhile, was planning to merge his forty-two thousand troops with General Don Carlos Buell's twenty thousand troops and wrest Corinth away from Confederate control.

On April 6, 1863, Johnston's soldiers attacked a Yankee patrol near the Shiloh Church. As the day wore on, Union troops were pushed back toward Pittsburg Landing on the Tennessee River. After General Buell's army arrived, the Confederate push was halted. The Confederates were delivered a stunning blow with the death of General Johnston, who bled to death after a bullet severed an artery in his leg. General Pierre G.T. Beauregard took command and was able to drive the Union army back two miles by the end of the day.

On April 7, Grant's troops forced the weary Confederates to retreat but suffered heavy casualties in the process. By nightfall, the Confederates were

The Confederate Memorial stands as a tribute to the more than ten thousand Confederate soldiers who died at the Battle of Shiloh. *Wikimedia Commons.*

forced to move back to Shiloh Church and eventually retreat to Corinth. Grant and Buell's armies suffered thirteen thousand casualties; over ten thousand Confederate soldiers were killed in the battle. The death toll at Shiloh was higher than that of any other battle fought in the country up to that time.

Accounts of paranormal activity at Shiloh National Battlefield have been reported for many years. The residual sounds of cannon fire, gunshots and drums echo across the battlefield at random times. In 2020, a man and his wife who were walking through the battlefield heard the pounding of hard-soled boots on the ground, as if someone were running past them. A few visitors have reported getting "up close and personal" with the ghosts of Shiloh. One visitor reported said that his T-shirt was pulled by invisible hands; another visitor claimed to have been hugged by a spectral presence.

Visitors to specific areas of the battlefield have experienced paranormal activity as well. One of these "haunt spots" is Bloody Pond. Because it was the only source of water on the battlefield, hundreds of Union and Confederate stopped there. Severely wounded and dying soldiers staggered over to the pond as well, hoping to enjoy a last sip of refreshing water and to clean their wounds. A number of these men were so weak that they were unable to raise their heads out of the pond after taking their last drink. By battle's end, the pond was bloody red in color. In their book *Haunted Battlefields of the South*, authors Bryan Bush and Thomas Freese tell the story of four tourists who walked over to Bloody Pond for a closer look. Within a matter of minutes, their faces were soaked in sweat, and they were overcome with nausea. Their symptoms vanished as soon as they were sitting inside their cars.

Another very haunted site on the battlefield is the Hornet's Nest, a name given by Braxton Bragg's attacking soldiers to General Benjamin M. Prentiss's defensive position. Twelve times, the Confederates were repulsed by the Federals' withering gunfire. Visitors to Shiloh report hearing cries and moans drifting in and around the Hornet's Nest, most likely the spirits of the brave men who were cut down by Prentiss's soldiers.

Even Shiloh Church, where General Sherman's men held their ground until driven back by the enemy, is said to have its share of spirits. One Sunday afternoon, a Civil War reenactor was walking around the church graveyard when he heard the sound of a wagon's creaking wheels and clanking chains. He walked over to the road for a better look, but the wagon was gone.

One of the ghost legends at Shiloh National Battlefield is the story of the drummer boy of Shiloh. In his book *Ghosts and Haunts of the Civil War*, author Christopher K. Coleman writes that on July 7, an unnamed drummer boy was ordered to sound the attack on the Confederate positions at Shiloh Church. However, as they neared the church, the Federal troops were met by a barrage of Confederate bullets, forcing them to halt their advance at the base of a sloping hill. Concerned that his men were about to be slaughtered, the Union officer ordered the drummer boy to play the drum call for "retreat." Instead, the drummer boy beat out "attack." When the officer asked the drummer boy why he had ignored his order, he replied, "Attack is the only drum call I know, sir." The officer's rage instantly turned to relief as Union troops forced their way up the hill, with bullets whizzing around their ears, and forced the Confederates to retreat. As soon as the smoke cleared, the officer began looking for the drummer boy so that he could commend him. To his dismay, the boy was dead, with a bullet in his heart.

With no historical proof as verification, this tale was considered by many to be apocryphal until the 1940s, when a construction crew working on a new road through the park discovered the skeletal remains of a child with a bullet lodged in the ribs that once protected the heart. Some visitors and reenactors believe that the spectral drummer boy is responsible for phantom drumbeats that occasionally echo across the battlefield.

Chapter 2

LEGENDARY BAD MEN

Cullen Baker: War Hero or Psychopath?

Weakly County

During and after the Civil War, the line between valiant defenders of the Lost Cause and murderous madmen was very thinly drawn. The most famous example of one of these men was Bloody Bill Anderson. As a member of Quantrill's Raiders, Anderson and the guerillas under his command participated in the massacre at Lawrence, Kansas, and the torture and murder of Union soldiers and sympathizers. Less well known, but equally bloodthirsty, was Cullen Baker.

The fourth of nine children, Cullen Baker was born on a farm in Weakley County, Tennessee, on June 23, 1835. When Baker was very young, he and his family moved to Clarksville, Arkansas. His father, John Baker, was respected far and wide as an honest farmer who worked hard raising crops and cattle. Cullen, on the hand, gained a reputation as a hothead early on. His fiery temper was said to become worse as he grew older, especially when he was drinking.

Baker gave every indication of wanting to settle down when he moved to Cass County, Texas, and married Martha Jane Sudduth. However, his fondness for alcohol and saloons continued. Eight months after his marriage, Baker was out carousing with several of his friends when he got into an argument with a young man named Stallcup. After exchanging insults, Baker grabbed a whip and nearly whipped Stallcup to death. Several men testified to Baker's brutal attack, and he was charged with the crime. However, before he could be tried, Baker went to the home of one of the witnesses, Wesley Bailey, and shot him point-blank with a shotgun, striking him in both legs. With the smoke still hanging in the air, Baker mounted his horse and rode off, leaving Bailey lying on the grass in front of his house. Baker rode back to Arkansas and holed up in a house owned by an uncle. Meanwhile, Baker's wife, Martha, gave birth to a baby girl on May 24, 1857. Three years later, Martha died. Baker returned to Texas long enough to bury his wife and farm out his daughter to relatives and then returned to Arkansas.

When he reached Arkansas, Baker soon discovered that his reputation for violence had preceded him. He flew into a rage when a woman named Beth Warthom started spreading around stories of his crimes. Baker gathered up a batch of hickory switches and marched over to Warthom's house. Before Baker could begin whipping Beth Warthom, her husband confronted Baker on the lawn and knocked him down. Watching from the doorway, Beth inadvertently distracted her husband by screaming. When he turned his head back toward the house, Baker produced a knife and stabbed him in the stomach, killing him. Once again, Baker fled the scene of the crime and returned to Texas, where he took another wife, Martha Foster.

The Civil War provided Baker with a refuge from the law and an outlet for his homicidal tendencies. He was credited with murdering three African Americans after they took the Oath of Allegiance in 1864. Later that year, he joined a branch of the Home Guard called the Independent Rangers, whose official mission was the apprehension of Confederate soldiers who had deserted. In reality, the Independent Raiders took advantage of the absence of the men who were off fighting against the Union army, leaving their families and property undefended. After eliminating competition from another band of vigilantes—the Mountain Boomers—the Independent Rangers attacked a group of people from Arkansas who were traveling to Texas. Baker murdered their leader and nine other men in what has become known as the Massacre of Saline. Toward the end of 1864, Baker joined a gang led by Lee Rames after shooting four African American Union soldiers. The Baker and Rames gang terrorized settlers living along the Sulphur River, robbing and murdering as many as thirty people.

By 1866, the Union army was in hot pursuit of Baker, forcing him to return once again to Texas, where his killer instincts had free rein. His victims included Private Albert E. Tutus; W.G. Kirman and John Salmons, who killed one of the members of Baker's gang; and George W. Barron, a member of the posse that was tracking Baker's gang. With a $1,000 bounty on his head, Baker fled to Arkansas, where he joined a mob that attacked the farm owned by a man who had hired several African Americans to work for him. The mob assaulted the farmer's two daughters but was driven back when the farmer began shooting at them. Baker was shot in the leg in the melee.

By 1869, Baker's uncontrollable temper was affecting his ability to lead the band of outlaws. Following a heated argument, Baker went off on his own with "Dummy" Kirby. They headed for the home of Baker's in-laws, where both men were killed. According to one theory, Baker's father-in-law offered the pair food and drink laced with strychnine. In another variant, his wife took a lover, a schoolteacher named Thomas Orr, during his extended absences. One night, Orr and a group of his friends caught up with the two men at the Fosters' home and gunned them down near the chimney.

Over time, the lives of American outlaws tend to be romanticized. Such is the case with the Cullen Baker, whom many people, including author Louis L'Amour, believed to be the first gunslinger. However, accounts from eyewitnesses indicate that Baker preferred to shorten the odds by using a shotgun instead of a pistol.

George "Machine Gun" Kelly Barnes

Memphis

George "Machine Gun" Kelly Barnes was born on July 18, 1895, in Memphis, Tennessee. The son of wealthy parents, Kelly gave no indication of criminal behavior. However, his reluctance to pursue the traditional career path for someone with his background surfaced in 1917 when he enrolled in Mississippi State University. He proved to be a poor student who earned demerits for constantly arguing with his professors. Kelly decided that it was time to grow up when he fell in love with and married Geneva Ramsey. He dropped out of Mississippi State University and went to work to support himself, his wife and their two children. He found work as a cab driver, but he did not earn enough to dig himself out of debt. When he was nineteen, he was unemployed, separated from his wife and desperate. He decided that the best way to make big money was bootlegging. Following several arrests, Kelly left Memphis with his new girlfriend and headed west. To insulate his family from the disgrace of having a gangster for a son, he began using the alias George R. Kelly. He was arrested and jailed several times before being incarcerated in Leavenworth Penitentiary for selling liquor on an Indian reservation in 1928. During his incarceration, he befriended several bank robbers, including Francis Keating and Thomas Holden, whom Kelly was suspected of aiding in their escape.

In 1929, Kelly was sentenced on a similar charge at the state penitentiary in New Mexico. Upon his release from prison, Kelly connected with a bootlegger named Steve Anderson. Before long, Kelly fell head-over-heels in love with Anderson's mistress, a former prostitute named Kathryn Thorne. The death of her husband, Charlie Thorne, was labeled a suicide, but the police suspected Kathryn may have "helped him along" somehow. Kathryn and Kelly got married in 1930.

Kathryn suspected that her small-time gangster husband had the potential to be much more. She bought him a machine gun and encouraged him to learn how to use it. She then began a public relations campaign to help Kelly gain entrance in underground circles. Legend has it that she walked into "drinking clubs" and placed spent cartridges on the tables. When the customers asked her why she was handing the cartridges out, she replied that they were souvenirs from "Machine Gun Kelly." Not only did Kathryn carefully cultivate her husband's "Machine Gun Kelly" image, but some historians believe that she might also have planned some of his bank robberies, as well. In 1933, the FBI's wanted posters portrayed the small-time bank robber as "Expert Machine Gunner."

Kelly was catapulted to national notoriety in July 1933 when he and Kathryn set up the kidnapping of an oil tycoon named Charles Urschel. One night, while Urschel was playing bridge with one of his friends, Kelly, carrying his machine gun, and two other men barged into Urschel's mansion. Kelly asked the men which one was Urschel. When neither of the men talked, Kelly ordered them both into his sedan. As they drove away, Kelly covered the men with a tarp and examined their billfolds. He discovered that one of them was named Walter Jarret. After dropping Jarret off on the side of an out-of-the way road, Kelly and his accomplices drove Urschel to a ranch in rural Texas. Kelly and Kathryn then demanded a ransom of $200,000 from Urschel's relatives.

On July 30, family friend E.E. Kirkpatrick made the ransom drop near the LaSalle Hotel in Kansas City. Urschel was released the next day near Norman, Oklahoma. Kelly and Kathryn split the ransom money with their accomplices. During his confinement, Urschel had made mental notes of the sounds he heard and the number of footsteps he heard while blindfolded. The police used this information to trace the location of the place where Urschel had been held to the ranch in Texas. They arrested one of the kidnappers using the serial numbers of the ransom money. Kelly and Kathryn tried to elude their pursuers by never staying in one state for very long. They also dyed their hair. They were on the lam for two weeks before deciding to return to Memphis, where they holed up with a friend named John Tichenor. On the morning of September 26, 1933, FBI agents forced their way into the Tichenor house with guns drawn. Kelly was lying on the couch, nursing a hangover. Rubbing his eyes, Kelly exclaimed, "G-men, please don't shoot!" Kathryn was in bed, asleep. Shortly thereafter, their accomplices were captured as well.

Kelly was taken to Leavenworth Prison, and Kathryn was placed in a federal prison in Cincinnati. After Kelly boasted that he would escape from Leavenworth, break his wife out of prison and spend Christmas with her, he was transferred to Alcatraz. His prison number was AZ#117. Warden Johnson remembered Kelly as being a model prisoner. Kelly worked in the laundry, served as an altar boy in the prison chapel and had a job in the industries office. He wrote voluminous letters to his family members and worried about Kathryn, whose sentence he believed was too harsh. Kelly was returned to Leavenworth in 1951 and died of a heart attack three years later. Following Kathryn's release from prison in 1958, she found employment as a bookkeeper at an Oklahoma hospital.

THE LAND PIRATE OF THE MISSISSIPPI: JOHN MURRELL

Williamson County

John Andres Murrell was an outlaw who terrorized settlers along the Mississippi River in the first half of the nineteenth century. Writer Mark Twain described the bandit known as "Reverend Devil" in his book *Life on the Mississippi* (1883), published one year after the death of Jesse James (1882): "Cheap histories of him [Jesse James] were on sale by train-boys. According to these, he was the most marvelous creature of his kind that had ever existed. It was a mistake. Murrell was his equal in boldness, in pluck, in rapacity; in cruelty, brutality, heartlessness, treachery, and in general and comprehensive vileness and shamelessness; and very much his superior in some larger aspects. James was a retail rascal; Murrell, wholesale." Born in Lunenburg County, Virginia, in 1806, Murrell moved to Williamson County, Tennessee, when he was very young. Murrell learned the Gospel from his father, a Methodist minister, but he also received informal training as a criminal while growing up. After stealing a horse in 1823, he was imprisoned for a year. Following his release, Murrell became the father of two children. In 1825, he began preaching around the Neutral Strip, a large area between the United States and Spanish-held territory in Texas. People said that after Murrell preached the word of the Lord, he helped himself to the cattle or personal belongings owned by the settlers he encountered in his travels. At the same time Murrell was spreading the Gospel of Jesus Christ, he was also organizing a gang of outlaws. He and his partners in crime had hideouts scattered in places like Midway Station and Los Adaes, but his headquarters was in a large cave near Kisatchie, Louisiana. Over time, his gang was divided into seven different clans, who used a secondary set of eight caves in western Sabine Parish as "banks." Because "cash money" was not used in this part of the country, much of their plunder consisted of gold and silver stolen from farmers and people traveling through the region. The outlaws identified themselves as members of a particular clan through the gold medallions they wore around their necks and by the black locust trees and dagger plants that they planted in their front yards.

Misconceptions about Murrell were fueled by Virgil A. Stewart's book *A History of the Detection, Conviction, Life and Designs of John A. Murrell, the Great Western Land Pirate.* In his book, Stewart accused Murrell of inciting slaves on plantations and then plundering the plantation houses during the ensuing chaos. The truth is, though, that none of Murrell's most unsavory schemes involved the stealing of slaves. He was said to have promised to help slaves escape and then resold them to someone else. In July 1834, he was convicted of slave stealing and sentenced to ten years' hard labor in prison. Nine years later, Murrell was released from prison after contracting tuberculosis. On November 1, 1844, Murrell succumbed to the disease in Pikeville, Tennessee.

John Murrell's legend survives in the stories that people still tell about his buried treasure. Many of the gang's hiding places were marked by carvings on rocks and trees. The largest of the caves used by the gang was in the Kisatchie National Forest. The discovery of a silver bar by a railroad worker near Sheard's Branch in 1924 intensified the search for Murrell's treasure. The U.S. Forest Service destroyed some of the gang's caves near Clearwater in Sabine Parish to prevent people from getting lost or injured. People still search for Murrell's gold, despite that fact many of the caves and the marked trees and rocks have been destroyed.

Robert Clay Allison

Wayne County

The fourth of nine children, Robert Clay Allison was born on a farm in Wayne County on September 2, 1841, to Mariah and Jeremiah Scotland Allison, a well-respected Presbyterian minister who raised crops and cattle. When the Civil War broke out in 1861, Allison traded in the life of farmer for the life of a horse soldier in Phillips's Tennessee Light Artillery Company in the Confederate army. He was accepted into the cavalry, even though he was born with a club foot. A head injury he suffered as a child made him prone to violent mood swings. Once, during a skirmish, he threatened to shoot his commanding officer if he did not order his men to fire on Federal troops as they retreated.

On January 15, 1862, Allison's mental instability led to his dismissal from the cavalry on a medical discharge. On September 22, 1862, Allison became a scout and spy for General Nathan Bedford Forest's Ninth Tennessee Cavalry. When his company surrendered at Gainesville, Alabama, on May 4, Allison became a prisoner of war. The night before he was to be executed on May 10, Allison broke out of prison.

The violent outbursts that became more frequent during the war continued to rule his life in peacetime. After returning home to Wayne County, Allison's temper got him into trouble on several different occasions, the most violent of which took place when a colonel from the Third Illinois Cavalry showed up at his mother's front door with orders to seize the family farm. In her attempt to throw the young man out of her house, a vase that her husband had given her as an anniversary present was broken. Alerted by the sounds of the struggle, Allison grabbed a rifle and shot the corporal.

Rather than face the consequences of his impulsive behavior, Allison, his brothers John and Monroe and his sister Mary and her husband moved out west in 1871. Allison's penchant for murder revealed itself in New Mexico when he learned about a deranged man named Charles Kennedy who was being held in jail on suspicion of being involved in the disappearance of his son and several strangers. Instead of waiting for the wheels of justice to turn, Allison formed a mob and stormed the jail, releasing the prisoner and hanging him. When the vigilantes searched Kennedy's house, they discovered the corpses of the man's son and the strangers.

In 1872, Allison started a ranch in Cimarron. Over time, he began frequenting saloons with the other cowboys. Not surprisingly, he got into a number of barroom brawls after a night of hard drinking. A friend of his named Mason Bowman helped Allisson refine his gunfighting skills. After he outdrew a gunman named Chunk Colbert and killed him, Allison became known as a dangerous man, especially when he was drinking. Many people believe that he might have participated in the mob hanging of Cruz Vega on October 30, 1875, for the murder of a Methodist circuit rider. Later, Allison killed Vega's uncle, Francisco Griego, in a gunfight. In January 1876, Allison got drunk and trashed the office of the Cimarron *News & Press* following the publication of an editorial attacking him. After sobering up, Allison paid $200 in damages. In December of that year, Allison and his brother John were drinking at a saloon in Las Animas, Colorado, when Constable Charles Faber ordered them to turn over their guns while they were in town. When the brothers refused, Faber stormed out of the bar. A few minutes later, he reappeared with two deputies, who opened fire on the pair. Allison was shot in the chest, arm and leg; he and his brother returned fire, killing Faber. Not surprisingly, the Allisons were charged with manslaughter, but the charges were later dropped on grounds of self-defense. In the spring of 1878, Allison was accused of aiding in the murder of three Black soldiers, but that charge was dropped as well.

In 1878, Allison decided that it was time to "pull up stakes" and move. After selling his ranch to his brother, John, for $700, Allison relocated to a plot of land on the Washita River and Gageby Creek. Two years later, Allison returned to ranching on property adjacent to land occupied by his sister Saluda Ann, her husband and several other transplants from Tennessee. Allison married Medora McCullough in 1881. The couple had two daughters, but seven months before the second child was born, Allison died. On July 3, 1887, Allison was hauling a wagon loaded with sacks of grain. When one of the grain sacks shifted, he attempted to catch it. Allison fell off of the wagon and was crushed to death when one of the wagon wheels rolled over his chest. He claimed that he "never killed a man that did not need killing." He was interred the next day in Pecos Cemetery. The epitaph on his tombstone reads, "Ironically, the man who received acclaim as one of the Old West's most fearsome gunslingers met his end, not in a gunfight, but in a vehicle accident."

When the Wildest of the Wild Bunch Came to Knoxville

Knoxville

Harvey Alexander Logan was born in Tama County, Iowa, in 1867. His mother, Eliza, died in 1876, leaving behind Harvey and his five siblings. Harvey and three of his brothers ended up in Texas, where Harvey took up the life of a cowboy. In 1883, he was on a cattle drive to Pueblo, Colorado, when he got into a fight in a saloon. With the law on his tail, Harvey took off for southern Wyoming. The next year found him homesteading a horse ranch in Chouteau County, Montana, with two of his brothers. On October 24, 1894, Harvey, his brother and his brother-in-law became involved in a heated argument with a miner named Powell Landusky, who accused Harvey of impregnating his daughter. Harvey settled the matter with his fists; afterward, he was charged with assault. The judge released Harvey at the inquest. However, when Harvey ran into the irate father in a saloon, Landusky drew a gun on Harvey. When the pistol misfired, Harvey returned fire, shooting Landusky in the head. Afterward, the girl admitted that Harvey's brother was the father of her baby, not Harvey.

Fearing that he would never get a fair trial, Harvey embarked on a life of crime. He returned to Montana, where he was confronted by a friend of Landusky's, James Winters. Guns were drawn; when the smoke cleared, Harvey's brother, Johnnie, lay dead on the ground. Harvey and his brother took off for New Mexico, where they joined up with Black Jack Ketchum's gang. Following a train robbery, Harvey and Lonnie joined another gang. While Harvey, Lonnie and the other gang members were rustling horses in April 1897, they were implicated in the shooting of Deputy Sheriff William Dean in Powder River, Wyoming. After fleeing to South Dakota, the bandits robbed a bank in Belle Fourche but were captured while making their getaway. They were incarcerated in Deadwood but escaped on October 31, 1897.

Harvey achieved his greatest notoriety when he joined up with the Wild Bunch. After participating in the robbery of a Southern Pacific locomotive in Humboldt, Nevada, in 1898, Harvey and the Wild Bunch robbed a Union Pacific Railroad overland flyer in Wilcox, Wyoming. Afterward, they sought refuge in the Hole in the Wall Pass near the Colorado/Utah border. Over the next two years, Harvey continued robbing trains and banks with different members of the Wild Bunch. During this time, two members of the gang—Lonnie Curry and "Flat Nose" George Curry—were shot and killed.

By 1901, Harvey Logan had become known as Kid Curry. He and the other members of the Wild Bunch had robbed the Great Northern Express near Wagner, Montana, so Harvey figured that it would be best to go someplace where nobody know him. In the summer of that year, Harvey adopted the alias William Wilson and moved to Knoxville, Tennessee. While he was seeing a young woman named Laura, he let it be known that he had made a considerable amount of money in "the railroad business." With the proceeds from his various robberies, Harvey bought a farm, where he hoped to live with Laura someday. Fate, though, had other plans for him. On December 13, 1901, the man who called himself Wilson was playing pool at Ike Jones's saloon. During the game, Wilson got into an altercation with one of pool players, a small-time crook named Luther Brady. At the time, two policemen, William Dinwiddie and Robert Saylor, were walking toward the saloon. The pair walked inside and tried to break up the scuffle. Dinwiddie grabbed Brady and arrested him. An instant later, Wilson fired his .38 Smith & Wesson at Saylor but missed. Both officers pulled out their billy clubs and began pummeling Wilson. Somehow, Harvey was able to shoot Saylor three times. Dinwiddie hit Harvey in the head so hard that he broke his billy club in half. Wilson shot Dinwiddie in the chest, but Dinwiddie still managed to wrest the gun from Harvey's hand. In the confusion, Wilson slipped out the back door.

When the police arrived, Saylor was lying on the pool table, and Dinwiddie was lying on the carpet. While the doctors treated their wounds, Deputy Sheriff Charles McCall and his bloodhounds tracked Wilson along a small creek to an abandoned bar in East Knoxville. It was here that the bloodhounds lost his trail. By Saturday morning, the inclement weather had made it impossible to resume the search.

Later that week, the police learned from some of the bystanders that Brady and two of the other pool players, James Boley and John Whipple, had seen Wilson pull some bills from a large roll in his pocketbook, so they concocted a plan to rob him. After Brady started a fight with Wilson, Boley and Whipple would steal his money. However, Brady, Boley and Whipple claimed that they found Wilson's pocketbook and arranged for Dennis Finley to take the money for them during the scuffle. The police discovered that the money in Finley's possession consisted of $3,680 in unsigned Bank of Montana bills. Convinced that he was one of the band of outlaws who taken part in the Great Northern Railroad robbery, they continued to search for the man whose true identity was unknown to them.

On Sunday, December 15, at 3:15 p.m., W.B. Carey informed the Knoxville police department that two suspicious-looking characters were sighted near the Jefferson Depot in Jefferson City. One of the men matched Wilson's description. While the Knoxville police headed to Jefferson, Carey organized a posse and began searching for Wilson. They found a man named John Drees walking along the railroad track toward Jefferson City. While two men stood guard over him, the rest of the search party continued looking for Wilson. They found him huddled over a campfire. He held up his hands and surrendered. He claimed that his name was Johnson. Around this time, several Knoxville policemen arrived in Jefferson City to take over the investigation. They searched Wilson and found $2,250 in Bank of Montana Bills. When Wilson was returned to Knoxville, a crowd of more than two thousand people was waiting to catch a glimpse of the prisoner. During the interrogation of Wilson, two patrolmen found $3,130 in Bank of Montana banknotes in Wilson's bags. Wilson denied that the bags were his.

The man who called himself Johnson tried to ingratiate himself with two of the policemen by giving one of them his gold watch and the other one an expensive ring.

At eight o'clock on Tuesday morning, Detective Lowell Spence from Knoxville arrived in Jefferson City. Following an examination of both prisoners, Spence informed Sheriff Fox that Drees was not involved in the Great Northern Railroad robbery but that Logan was actually Harvey Logan. Harvey was returned to Knoxville to stand trial. In November 1902, the jury convicted him of counterfeiting and forgery. Before the United States Circuit Court of Appeals could arrive at a decision, Harvey broke out of the Knox County jail on June 27, 1903. Rumors soon spread that the prisoner had bribed a deputy to help him escape, but they were never confirmed.

The next year, Harvey Logan's outlaw career came to a violent end. He and a number of other bad men robbed the Denver & Rio Grande train near Parachute, Colorado, on June 9, 1904. A posse apprehended the men two days later. A gunfight ensued, and Harvey was severely wounded. Rather than spend the rest of his life in prison, Harvey opted to die by suicide.

Chapter 3

LEGENDARY CEMETERIES

Craigmiles Mausoleum

Cleveland

Most people, especially parents, would probably agree that nothing is sadder than the death of a child. This might be the reason why so many of these tragic occurrences have been memorialized in ghost stories. One of these mournful specters is the spirit of Nina Craigmiles. She was born in 1864 to Adelia Thompson, the daughter of a local physician, and John Henderson Craigmiles, a merchant who had made a fortune selling supplies to prospectors during the California gold rush. Craigmiles also capitalized on the urgent need for supplies during the Civil War. He and his wife spoiled Nina shamelessly, showering the little girl with all of the toys and clothes that their wealth could provide.

The family's happiness came to an abrupt end on a chilly October day in 1871. Nina's grandfather, Dr. Thompson, pulled his buggy up in front of his daughter's house, just as he had done so many times before. He knocked on the door, and seven-year-old Nina ran out of the house and rushed into his arms. As they rode along, the doctor noticed that the horses were not responding to his commands. He turned the buggy around and was heading home when the railroad crossing came into view. He ordered the horses to slow down, but they ignored him, galloping faster instead. Just as the horses cleared the tracks, a train collided with the buggy, smashing

John and Adelia Craigmiles built St. Luke's Episcopal Church and the mausoleum behind it in memory of their daughter, Nina. *Wikimedia Commons.*

it to pieces. Dr. Thompson was thrown clear and survived with just a few minor injuries; Nina, unfortunately, died instantly.

John and Adelia were devasted by the loss of their little girl. Instead of wallowing in their grief, they decided to erect a church to perpetuate Nina's memory. St. Luke's Episcopal Church was hailed as one of the finest Episcopal cathedrals in Tennessee. Nina's beautiful white mausoleum was erected behind the church. A few months later, Adelia gave birth to a second baby, a boy, but he died only a few hours after birth. His small body was placed inside the mausoleum alongside Nina's body. Sadly, tragedy continued to plague the Craigmiles family. In 1899, John Craigmiles was walking on the sidewalk downtown when he slipped on a patch of blue ice and fell down. A few days later, he died of blood poisoning. His body was placed inside Nina's mausoleum. Adelia married a respectable member of the community named Charles Cross and had a good life until she was crossing the street one day and a car struck and killed her. In accordance with her wishes, she, too, was interred in the mausoleum.

For years, locals have believed that the Craigmiles's grief has imprinted itself on the mausoleum. Shortly after Nina was placed inside the mausoleum, the caretaker noticed red splotches on one of the sides. It was still wet, so he washed it off with a rag. The next day, however, the red splotches returned. Wiping away the red splotches became a daily ritual for the caretaker, who discovered that with the passing of time, the splotches became more and more difficult to remove until, finally, they left stains. After a while, more stains appeared on the side of the building. Not surprisingly, locals began referring to the structure as the "Bleeding Mausoleum." For many years, visitors to the church have seen the ghost of a little girl, dressed in Victorian-era clothes, playing outside of the mausoleum, forever locked in her childhood.

Elmwood Cemetery

Memphis

Located at 824 South Dudley Street, Elmwood Cemetery was founded in 1852 by fifty wealthy investors who paid $500 for a single share of Elmwood Cemetery Association stock. The name of the cemetery was chosen in a lottery. Several proposed names for the new cemetery were placed in a hat. "Elmwood Cemetery" was selected as the winner. The cemetery was laid out on eighty acres of land located two miles outside of the Memphis city limits.

Over seventy thousand people have been buried in Elmwood Cemetery: the famous, the infamous and ordinary citizens of Memphis. People say that the ghosts of some of the "dear departed" have not really left the cemetery. A case in point occurred in 1982. In her book *Haunted Memphis*, author Laura Cunningham writes of a weird experience a caretaker had when he was closing up the cemetery around nightfall. As he was walking across the grounds, he saw four men dressed in white top hats and suits standing on top of a hill, engaged in conversation. Cunningham suggests that these men might have been the ghosts of four of the most important men in the city—David Park Hadden, Napoleon Hill, Henry A. Montgomery and Archibald Wright—who met on the corner of Madison Street every morning to discuss current affairs. They seem to be continuing their conversations after death.

A caretaker at Elmwood Cemetery saw the apparition of four men in white top hats and suits at the top of a hill. *Wikimedia Commons.*

The ghost of one of the city's most notorious residents is also active in the afterlife. In January 1892, nineteen-year-old Alice Mitchell walked down to the steamboat landing to say goodbye to her friend, seventeen-year-old Frederica "Freda" Ward. At least, that was the reason Alice gave the authorities for the meeting. As Alice approached Freda, she pulled out her father's straight razor from her dress and slit Freda's throat. Up until that moment, no one in town realized that the girls were having a clandestine affair. During the trial, Alice testified that she loved Freda so much that she wanted the girl to die before she did. The jury found her "presently insane" and sentenced her to confinement in the state mental institution. Alice died there in 1898. Visitors to her grave in Elmwood Cemetery have found that every photograph they have tried to take of her tombstone has turned out blurred. Alice Mitchell, it seems, really values her privacy.

Fort Donelson National Cemetery

Dover

Fort Donelson surrendered to General Ulysses S. Grant's forces on Sunday, February 16, 1862. In 1863, the Union army constructed a fort on the site of the abandoned Confederate works. Before long, a freedman's community grew up around the new fort. In 1867, the Fort Donelson National Cemetery was established here. The first burials were the remains of 670 Union soldiers who had been previously buried on the battlefield, in local cemeteries, in hospital cemeteries and in nearby towns. Of the 670 Union soldiers buried there, 5 of the known and 9 of the unknown soldiers were from the United States Colored Troops. Fort Donelson National Cemetery has an unusually large number of unknown soldiers because most soldiers at this time did not carry personal identification. Also, because the burial details were under pressure to clean up the battlefield as quickly as possible, no time was allotted to identify the bodies. After the Civil War, Fort Donelson National Cemetery became the final resting place for veterans who served in the U.S. Armed Forces since the Civil War as well.

The spirit of one of the soldiers who were interred in Fort Donelson National Cemetery is named Reuben Hammond. Visitors who encounter his apparition feel that he is a sad and lonely spirit who keeps watch over the

The spirit of a fallen soldier named Reuben Hammond guards the bodies of his comrades in arms at Fort Donelson National Cemetery. *Wikimedia Commons.*

cemetery to guard the bodies of his fallen comrades. Some visitors have felt his presence follow them around as they look at the names on the tombstones. People who made his acquaintance in the cemetery claim to have seen him wave goodbye from the high ground of the cemetery.

One woman who visited the cemetery had some very strange experiences during her stay there. Eager to see if there was any truth to the ghost stories she had heard, she held an EVP session inside the cemetery. When she played back the recording she had made, she distinctly heard a spectral voice say "No" in response to one of the questions she asked. She also heard footsteps down in the ravine. When she walked over to the edge of the ravine to investigate, she found nothing that could have made that particular sound. Needless to say, the spectral "No" in the recording did not change her mind regarding paranormal activity at Fort Donelson National Cemetery.

Nashville City Cemetery

Nashville

Nashville City Cemetery is the oldest graveyard in Tennessee. The cemetery was established in 1822. Its abundant greenery and twisting paths give visitors the feeling that they are walking through a park. By 1850, approximately eleven thousand people had been buried there. Over time, the old cemetery suffered from neglect. Then, in the late 1950s, the mayor of Nashville, Ben West, initiated the restoration of the historic burial ground. Within a decade, the cemetery had improved so much that it was added to the National Register of Historic Places. Like many historic cemeteries in the South, Nashville City Cemetery is the final resting place of influential politicians and Confederate generals; unlike many historic southern cemeteries, however, Nashville City Cemetery is integrated. Black and white, rich and poor lie side by side. Visitors are as likely to find important figures in the city's history as they are to find slaves and carpenters.

One would expect a graveyard as old as the Nashville City Cemetery to be haunted, and according to fans of anything paranormal, it certainly is. One of the haunted sites in the cemetery is the grave of attorney Charles Dickinson. On May 30, 1806, Dickinson fought a duel with Andrew Jackson. Fully aware of Jackson's history of dueling, Dickinson aimed at his opponent's chest and fired, missing his target. Jackson, who was a much better shot—and faster, as well—killed Dickinson. People who have visited

Dickinson's grave site have reported cold chills seeping over them, even on hot days. Some visitors report being touched by unseen fingers near the grave and feeling as if someone is watching them.

This portrait of Andrew Jackson was painted by Ralph E.W. Earle. The ghost of Charles Dickinson, an attorney killed by Andrew Jackson in a duel, is said to touch visitors to his grave. *Wikimedia Commons.*

The most famous grave in the Nashville City Cemetery is the grave of Ann Rawlins Sanders, who died in 1836 when she was only twenty-one years old. Locals say that one day, she and her husband got into a heated argument. After Ann "had her say," she screamed at her husband and stormed out of the house. Ann walked around the town in a daze for a while before finding herself standing on a cliff overlooking the river. Overcome with depression and loneliness, she plunged into the river below and drowned. When her husband learned of Ann's fate, he was wracked with feelings of guilt and sadness. After the period of mourning was over, he went out to the site of his wife's suicide and cut off a large section of the cliff that she stood on just before her death. He then moved the piece of cliff to Ann's grave. Know that she had a fear of the dark, he fastened a lantern at the top of the grave. Visitors to her grave have heard the faint sounds of a woman weeping and arguing with someone. Her apparition has been sighted sitting on top of the boulder with her head in her hands. She has also been seen sitting near the boulder with the ghost of a man wearing clothes from the early nineteenth century. It seems that Ann has found the companionship she longed for when she was alive.

Old Gray Cemetery

Knoxville

Founded in 1850, Old Gray Cemetery was named for the British poet Thomas Gray, who wrote the poem "Elegy in a Country Churchyard." The cemetery greatly increased its size when it was joined with the Knoxville National Cemetery. Union general Ambrose Burnside decided to merge the two cemeteries to provide burial space for his soldiers occupying Knoxville.

The Horne Monument stands over the graves of Confederate soldiers William and John Horne at Old Gray Cemetery. It is marked by the statue of a Confederate with his back turned toward the Union Monument. *Wikimedia Commons.*

Old Gray Cemetery is said to be haunted by a figure in a dark robe called a "Black Aggie." According to Lewis Powell IV, author of the Southern Spirit Guide article "Old Gray Cemetery," the legend of the Black Aggie has its source in a statue carved by sculptor Augustus Saint-Gaudens for the Adams Memorial in Rock Creek Cemetery, Washington, D.C. A copy of the statue, which depicts a figure representing grief, was copied and sold to General Felix Agnus in Pikesville, Maryland. The statue was moved to the garden of the Dolley Madison House in Washington. Other copies of the statue, and the legend they inspired, can be found in cemeteries all over the world. The Black Aggie in Old Gray Cemetery has been seen wandering around, looking for something—or someone.

In the 2009 book *Haunted Tennessee*, this author wrote of the experience that a couple of teenage legend trippers had in the Old Gray Cemetery. While waiting for the Black Aggie to appear, they were drinking beer. Fueled by alcohol, the pair decided to provoke the spirit by cussing and urinating on one of the tombstones. Suddenly, a black mass oozed from one of the graves and took human form. Then the entity started coming toward the young men. Screaming, they ran to their car and jumped in. Just before their vehicle tore out of the cemetery, one of the young men stuck his camera out of the window and took a quick picture. Supposedly, they have refused to show the photograph to anyone else.

According to Laura Still, a tour guide for Knoxville Walking Tours, the graveyard may also be haunted by the ghosts of two artists from Knoxville, Catherine Wiley and her mentor, Lloyd Branson. The artists, who painted in the impressionistic style, were rumored to have become lovers at some point in their professional relationship. Apparently, their romantic affair has persisted into the afterlife. "They meet sometimes, maybe for a moonlight stroll," Still said. "They've been spotted hand-in-hand at twilight, so it's kind of nice."

Another female spirit, author Virginia Rosalie Coxe, has a far different reason for haunting Old Gray Cemetery. The regional author of a number of popular works in the 1890s, Coxe died of kidney disease at a relatively young age. In 2010, the memory of the nineteenth-century writer was revived following an act of vandalism to her statue. Legend has it that Coxe's restless spirit roams the cemetery, looking for her hand. According to Laura Still, the missing hand was located several years later and will eventually be reattached to her statue. "If you meet her, tell her the board has it," Still said.

Red Ash Cemetery/Turley Cemetery

Caryville

Red Ash Cemetery (also known as Turley Cemetery) is all that remains of a mining town that flourished in Campbell County from the mid-1800s up through the 1950s. The size of the little cemetery increased considerably in the 1930s when a number of burials were reinterred there during the 1934 Norris Dam Grave Relocation Project. Today, the historic cemetery, which lies on an unmarked road off Old Highway 43, bears the unmistakable signs of neglect and vandalism. Nevertheless, its reputation as one of the most haunted cemeteries in Tennessee has made it a favorite with legend trippers and ghost hunters.

Many of the tales about Red Ash Cemetery originated with young curiosity seekers who ventured out to the secluded spot to party, to prove their courage and, hopefully, to have a brush with the paranormal. Sightings include the ghost of a woman crying over her own grave and a black-robed figure called a Black Aggie. Eerie blue lights have been seen flitting around the tombstones. A goat-like creature is rumored to be guarding the gates of the cemetery. Many of the locals believe that the spirits of their friends and relatives who are buried there walk around the graveyard at night. Some locals say that anyone who removes coins placed in the hands of the angel statue in the cemetery will have bad luck. One young man who went to Red Ash Cemetery at night with some friends claimed to have heard a strange howling sound that seemed to be part man and part wolf. On another night, they saw four red eyes glaring at them from the darkness.

Many paranormal groups who have checked out the cemetery have not gone away empty-handed. A number of these investigators have recorded startling EVPs there at night. Hopefully, anyone who visits Red Ash Cemetery will treat it with the respect that hallowed ground deserves. After all, the people who rest there have relatives who still love them and remember them.

Chapter 4

LEGENDARY LOCATIONS

Bijou Theatre

Knoxville

The building that houses the Bijou Theatre is the third-oldest structure in Knoxville. When it was built in 1817, it housed Archie Ray's Tavern. By the time of the Civil War, it had become the Lamar House hotel. During the war, the hotel served as both a military hospital and a barracks for Union officers. The field hospital's most famous patient was General William P. Sanders, who had been shot by a Confederate sniper. He died in the former bridal suite in 1863. After passing through several owners, part of the building was converted into Jake Wells's Bijou Theatre. For the next two decades, a number of vaudeville acts performed here, including the Marx Brothers and Al Jolson. After vaudeville died, the theater began showing movies. The Bijou Theatre entered a period of decline in the 1930s. Then, in the 1960s, it became an art house for X-rated adult movies. After the theater closed, it was renovated in the 1970s and reopened as a center for the performing arts.

Not long after the theater reopened, staff and actors began noticing odd occurrences, usually after the theater closed for the day. One day, an office worker was closing up when he noticed a little girl standing in the lobby. When he approached the child, she vanished. The balcony is believed to be haunted by two ghosts, one who stands in the front rows of the first balcony

The ghost of a stagehand named Ellum Smiley may be responsible for dirt and plaster falling down on the stage during a rehearsal at the Bijou Theatre. *Wikimedia Commons.*

and another who has been sighted on the second floor. The best-known ghost is the spirit of General Sanders, whose apparition wanders through the entire theater. One evening, a member of the cleaning staff, Sharlene Bousch, was working by herself. She had just cleaned the ladies' room and was opening the door to the men's room when she saw a man wearing a uniform with gold buttons. She got out of there as fast as she could.

Tim Burns, the former technical director, recalls standing in the grid area in 1986 when he heard a loud crash. Suddenly, plaster and dirt started falling from the ceiling area. He looked up, but no one was walking around up there. He suspected that the ghost of a stagehand named Ellum Smiley might have been responsible. Smiley's signature is still visible on one of the rafters.

In an interview with WBIR 10 News, author Laura Still traced some of the haunted activity inside the theater to 1876, when the manager of the Lama Hotel, Thomas Sneed, got into an argument with Thomas Atkins, manager of the Atkins Hotel. Both men had been drinking heavily at an all-day party at the Lamar House. At three o'clock in the morning, Atkins became angry because no one in the Lamar House would serve him a glass of water. When Sneed asked Atkins why he wanted water instead of a "man's drink," the men began shoving each other. When Atkins caught a glimpse of Sneed's derringer inside his coat, he slammed Sneed to the floor. Sneed rose from the floor and shot Atkins, killing him. Because Sneed claimed self-defense, he was never charged with Atkins's murder. Still says that the phantom footsteps people hear inside the theater are an indication that Thomas Atkins is still looking for a glass of water.

Not surprisingly, the Bijou Theatre has been a favorite "haunting spot" with ghost hunters. In 2006, an all-night investigation by an East Mississippi paranormal group captured some very compelling, if not conclusive, evidence of ghostly activity. On the fourth floor, the members recorded EVPs of people talking. On the second-floor balcony and in the ladies' room, they filmed several shadowy figures and the ghost of a little girl, as well as a number of orbs. Using infrared video, the members filmed the faces of actors in costume. It seems that the ghosts of the Bijou Theatre are finding it difficult to stop performing, even in the afterlife.

Cades Cove

Gatlinburg

According to legend, Cades Cove, a four-thousand-acre valley in Great Smoky Mountains National Park, is named after Chief Cade, a Cherokee Indian chief. In 1794, Hugh Dunal received a land grant of five thousand acres in Cades Cove. However, because the Cherokees did not cede the land to the settlers until the signing of the Treaty of Calhoun in 1819, attacks by angry Cherokees were a real threat until they were relocated west of the Mississippi on the Trail of Tears in 1830. One of the early settlers in Cades Cove received aid from friendly Cherokees when he and his wife, Lucretia, built their cabin in 1818. William Tipton and his two brothers, Abraham and Thomas, moved to Cades Cove in 1821 and eventually owned some of the best farming land in the area. By 1850, 671 people were living in Cades Cove. Many of them were farmers who cleared the land and grew corn, for the most part. They also hunted deer and raised hogs. During the Civil War, the sympathies of the settlers were divided between the Union and the Confederacy. Confederate bushwhackers wreaked havoc in Cades Cove, killing Union sympathizers and stealing supplies. Many of the people who fled Cades Cove during the war never came back. The population of Cades Cove was on the decline by the end of the 1800s, until logging

The apparition of a woman has been seen outside the Primitive Baptist Church at Cades Cove. *Alan Brown.*

replaced farming in the early 1900s as the primary occupation. Many people in Cades Cove depended on moonshine corn liquor as an extra source of income. Determined to transform Cades Cove into a national park, the U.S. government confiscated the land in the 1920s, forcing most of the residents to abandon their property.

Today, thousands of tourists, drawn to the settlement's primitive beauty and serenity, drive the eleven miles around Cades Cove Scenic Loop. Over time, a number of myths and legends arose about the area. For example, a few visitors have heard that the "smoke" encircling the peaks of the Smoky Mountains is produced by fog machines, despite the fact that scientists have proven that the fog is produced by the millions of trees and bushes in the region. A number of people believe that the park releases 1,500 black bears in the morning. Some die-hard believers claim that cougars still show up in the park occasionally; however, the historical record states that the cougars in the Smoky Mountains were eradicated in the late 1800s. All of the sightings of cougars in recent years are either hoaxes or misidentified animals like coyotes or bobcats.

Ghost stories are the most prevalent legends being passed around Cades Cove in the twenty-first century. One of these tales centers on the Primitive Baptist Church. Pioneer John Oliver was one of the founders of Cades Cove Baptist Church in 1827. In 1839, following a split in the church, it was renamed Cades Cove Primitive Baptist Church. The current church building replaced the early log church. Locals say that people walking around the side of the present church after dusk have seen the apparition of a woman. Supposedly, someone has taken a photograph of a woman's face on the wall of one of the historic churches in Cades Cove.

One of the most frightening stories to come out of Cades Cove is the legend of the "cussing cover." This particular variant was recounted in Janet Marnett's book *The Granny Curse and Other Ghosts and Legends from East Tennessee*. Back in the nineteenth century, Basil and Mavis Estep were living in a two-room cabin. Mavis, who was born in a thunderstorm, was paranoid about being struck by lightning someday. Because of her phobia, Mavis refused to sleep in a metal bed. Ironically, Mavis was taken down not by a thunderbolt but by disease. As she was lying on her deathbed, she made Basil promise that he would never sell any of the quilts she had made herself and that

The legend of the cussing cover takes place in a cabin similar the Dan Lawson Place in Cades Cove. *Alan Brown.*

he would never cover a metal bed with any of her beloved quilts. A few months after Mavis died, Basil married a much younger woman, Trulie Jane Lawson, and brought her to the cabin where he and Mavis had spent so many happy years together. Because Mavis's wooden frame bed was too small for Trulie Jane, she and Basil slept on a metal bed. One cold night, Trulie Jane persuaded Basil to allow her to cover the bed with one of Mavis's quilts. She selected a quilt that Basil called the cussing cover because Mavis had made it with part of a shirt Basil was wearing when the couple had their first argument. During the night, Trulie Jane and Basil were fast asleep when a bolt of lightning streaked through one of the windows and struck the metal bed, knocking Trulie Jane to the floor. When the stunned woman rose to her feet, she was horrified by what she saw: the metal bed was completely destroyed, and the charred corpse of her husband was stretched out on the floor. For some reason, the cussing cover was perfectly intact. People say that a local collector in the Smokies purchased the cursed quilt. No one knows where the cussing cover is now.

Drummond Bridge Trestle

Briceville

In the early 1890s, the Coal Creek Mining and Manufacturing Company embarked on a plan to save money by using prisoners from the Tennessee state prison system to mine coal. This decision on the part of mine owners left many local coal miners in Briceville unemployed. Tempers reached a fever pitch on October 31, 1891, when the coal miners armed themselves and revolted against the mining company. Governor John P. Buchanan sent the militia to Briceville to quell the conflict. As a result, the convict lease system was abolished, but men on both sides lost their lives. One of the casualties was a twenty-five-year-old former sailor named Dick Drummond. In 1893, Drummond killed a young soldier named William Laugherty in a dispute over a girl. His fellow militiamen retaliated by hanging Drummond from the train trestle. He was the only miner who was killed by the governor's soldiers.

Drummond's unquiet spirit still haunts the site of his murder. Curiosity seekers claim to have seen his shadowy apparition hanging from the bridge's trestlework. Some legend trippers claim to have seen Drummond's ghost walking the tracks from one end of the bridge to the other. Drummond's mournful cries have been heard on and around the bridge as well. Some locals say that dogs will not venture near the bridge and cattle will not graze under the tracks. Folklorists would say that Dick Drummond will continue to be a restless spirit because justice was never served.

Earnestine and Hazel's

Memphis

The building that houses Earnestine and Hazel's was built in the late 1800s as a church. In the early twentieth century, it housed a pharmacy and general store. The story goes that after the pharmacist created Coppertone and made a fortune, he sold everything to the two hairdressers with whom he had shared the building, a couple of cousins named Earnestine and Hazel. Hazel's husband, a concert promoter, converted the building into a getaway where musicians like Chuck Berry, Ike Turner and B.B. King could relax after a performance. Eventually, a side business—prostitution—opened up in the rooms upstairs. In 1997, on St. Patrick's Day, Russell George bought the business and transformed it into a nightspot offering beer and "soul burgers." Hazel died in 1995, and Earnestine followed her in death in 1998.

Before long, tales of the spirits inside the building added to the bar's allure. One of the most haunted features of Earnestine and Hazel's is the jukebox. Its tendency to turn on by itself could be the result of faulty wiring. However, the fact that some of the songs it plays on its own pertain to conversations people are having at the time is not as easy to explain away. For example, a small group of men were discussing exorcisms when the Rolling Stones' song "Sympathy for the Devil" started playing on the jukebox. On a different occasion, a couple of employees were talking about James Brown on the day he died when the jukebox started playing Brown's song "I Feel Good." The spirits of the former bordello interact with customers in different ways as well. Patrons on the upper floor have seen shadowy figures in the hallways and heard the sound of a piano playing and disembodied voices. A server was checking out one night when she was touched by an invisible hand. Orbs have appeared in many of the photographs taken upstairs. One evening, an employee who had worked there for fifteen years went upstairs. A few minutes later, he ran down the stairs, through the bar and out the door. He never explained what had scared him so much that he could not work there anymore.

In July 2019, workers began renovating the bar and dance floor. Late one afternoon, a work crew was repairing a wall when, to their surprise, several bones fell out of a hole they had made. At eleven o'clock that night, police and firemen converged on the historic building. In addition to the bones, the emergency teams also found a box containing several old bottles. Later, the bones were sent off for identification. While the restoration was underway, Earnestine and Hazel's operated out of the back of the bar. One wonders if the improvements made in the old building have made the ghosts even more active.

Falcon Rest

McMinnville

Clay Faulkner's beautiful home was built in the Queen Anne architectural style in 1896 and 1897. Faulkner's father, Asa Faulkner, was a well-to-do mill owner and politician. Following his father's example, Clay Faulkner became the owner of the Great Falls Cotton Mill, which manufactured heavy-duty apparel called Gorilla Pants. Faulkner told his wife, the former Mary King Saunders, that he would build her "the grandest mansion in Tennessee" if she would agree to live next to the factory. She agreed, and the couple lived at Falcon Rest with their five children for many years. Between 1929 and 1941, the house served as Dr. Herman Reynolds's private residence and office. Mayor W.V. Jones lived at Falcon Rest from 1943 to 1945. In 1945, a nursing home operated on the first floor of the house. In 1948, a hospital opened on the second floor. Operations were performed in one of the children's rooms on the second floor. The nursing home and hospital closed in 1968. In 1989, George McGlothin bought the former nursing home and hospital at auction with the intention of restoring it. Falcon Rest has been a bed-and-breakfast since 1993.

George McGlothin believes that the spirit of the original owner, Clay Faulkner, is responsible for many of the strange occurrences in the historic house. Faulkner, who died in a first-floor bedroom in 1916, makes his presence known by moving objects to different places in the house. Guests can also tell when he is around by the pungent smell of cigar smoke. Faulkner's spirit may have inadvertently frightened a young man who was decorating a Christmas tree in the upstairs hallway. He was whistling "It Came Upon a Midnight Clear" while he was hanging ornaments. When he finished decorating, he stopped whistling and was walking down the stairs when he heard someone else whistling the same Christmas carol. Terrified, the young man rushed over to the visitors' center, where he told of his encounter with the late Mr. Faulkner.

The mill owner's ghost is not the only spirit haunting Falcon Rest. Liz, one of the tour guides, was talking to a group in Faulkner's bedroom when a visitor asked if the woman she saw dressed in Victorian clothing was a reenactor. Puzzled, Liz replied that there were no reenactors inside Falcon Rest on that particular day. Liz continued with her story about Faulkner's ghost when she was interrupted by a loud crashing sound coming from the dining room. When she ran into the room, Liz was surprised to find the ornate antique mirror lying on the floor. Amazingly, the glass was unbroken, and the wire and screws were still attached to the wall. Since that incident occurred, the owners have removed the mirror, but the screws are still securely anchored to the wall.

Other types of ghostly activity have been reported at Falcon Rest as well. Guests have occasionally felt waves of cold air waft over them. A film crew

The ghostly face of Clay Faulkner's mother-in-law has been sighted staring out of a second-floor window at Falcon Rest Bed and Breakfast. *Alan Brown.*

from the local PBS station heard a loud burst of static when the recording was played back. Mrs. McGlothlin has detected the phantom smell of cigar smoke in the library on the second floor. The day before a wedding, the groom spent in the night in a second-floor room the children called the Slopey Room because of the sloping ceiling. The next morning, he reported that he heard the sounds of children running around the room all night long. Several years ago, an elderly woman nicknamed Granny lived in Clay Faulkner's bedroom for two years. During this time, she frequently heard heavy footsteps walk down the stairway and stop outside of the bedroom door. She believed that this was Clay Faulkner's way of letting her know that he would be watching out for her until morning. The spirit of an older woman wearing a bow in her hair and an old-fashioned dress with a high neckline has been seen staring out of one of the bedroom windows on the second floor. In 1997, a group of paranormal investigators captured the photographic image of a face in the mirror in Faulkner's bedroom. Most of the time, the guests are frightened not by the spirits themselves but by the unexpected nature of the occurrences, which could be the work of spirits whose names are unknown or the ghost of one of the many people who died there back when the building served as a hospital.

Graceland

Memphis

On March 25, 1957, Elvis Presley took a break from the filming of *Loving You* to travel to Memphis and purchase a ten-thousand-square-foot mansion from Ruthie Brown Moore for $102,500. Built with tan Tennessee limestone, Presley's new home was a far cry from the little shotgun shack in Tupelo, Mississippi, where he was born on January 8, 1935. Eager to add his own touches to his new home, Elvis installed the music gates less than a month after he bought the property. He also increased the size of the mansion by seven thousand square feet. For Elvis, Graceland was his personal castle, befitting the "King of Rock and Roll."

The adoration of Elvis's millions of fans would not let him die, even after he suffered a fatal heart attack on July 20, 1977. The rumor that Elvis had faked his death because he was tired of living under a microscope led to hundreds of Elvis sightings all over the country. These reports differ dramatically from the Elvis sightings at Graceland. Because Elvis spent some

Above: Reports of ghostly activity at Graceland surfaced soon after the mansion was opened to the public on June 7, 1982. *Alan Brown.*

Left: A girl who was looking at one of Elvis's white jumpsuits saw his face in the glass case. *Alan Brown.*

of the happiest years of his life here, it stands to reason that this is where his ghost would return.

The ghostly sightings of Elvis began shortly after Graceland was opened to the public as a museum on June 7, 1982. Within just a few months, visitors reported seeing his ghost sitting behind a screen door in the back of the house and standing in a first-floor and a second-floor window. Many people claim to have seen him seated in a black limousine as it exits Graceland at night. In his book *Ghosts and Haunts of Tennessee*, author Christopher Coleman writes of a girl's encounter with the ghost of Elvis while she was gazing at a one of his white jumpsuits in a display case. She said that she caught a fleeting glimpse of Elvis's face in the glass.

Another young person to whom Elvis appeared was a sixteen-year-old girl. According to the book *Ghost Stories of Tennessee* by A.S. Mott, the girl was touring Graceland with her parents when, suddenly, she had to go to the bathroom. She detached herself from the group that was listening with rapt attention to the tour guide and wandered off in search of a bathroom. She finally found one that seemed to be off-limits to the general public, but she was desperate, so she opened the door and walked inside. After she took care of business, she was standing at the sink, washing her hands, when she noticed the reflection of a man dressed like Elvis Presley in the mirror. He was standing behind her. She started to apologize to the man when, suddenly, he disappeared. The girl quickly rejoined the group and told everyone about seeing Elvis in the bathroom. Goosebumps rose on her arm when the tour guide informed her that she had been in the bathroom where Elvis died.

On another occasion, a photographer for a nationally known magazine was sent to Graceland to photograph the mansion. After he completed his assignment, he flew back to New York. As he was examining the developed photographs, he was dismayed to see that all of them were overexposed and useless. However, he felt a glimmer of hope when, in the corner of the last photograph, he saw the spectral image of the face of Elvis Presley. At that moment, he realized that this one photograph was more valuable than clear photographs of the mansion would have been. Unfortunately, both the negative and the photograph were destroyed in freak accidents. It seemed to the photographer that maybe Elvis did not want his picture taken.

Other ghosts have been sighted outside of Graceland as well. A girl was standing outside of the mansion, looking at the horse barn, when she saw a black horse run across the pasture and enter the barn. She learned from the audio tour that Elvis's favorite horse was a black stallion named Jack. The girl's eyes opened wide when she was told that no horses were in the barn on

A young woman saw the ghost of Elvis's favorite horse, a black stallion named Jack, gallop across the pasture and run inside the barn. *Alan Brown.*

that particular day. The ghost of Elvis's mother, Gladys, who died on August 14, 1958, has been sighted gazing out of the kitchen window and walking down the hallway leading to her son's bedroom, singing a gospel song. At Graceland, the past is celebrated and—at times—relived.

The Hermitage

Nashville

Long before moving into the residence that is generally associated with the seventh president of the United States, Andrew Jackson and his wife, Rachel, lived on farm called Poplar Grove between 1792 and 1796. The couple then moved to another farm, Hunter's Hill, on the Cumberland River. Jackson had to sell Hunter's Hill after one of his business partnerships fell through. He then purchased a smaller, 425-acre plantation from his neighbor on July 5, 1804. For the next fifteen years, the Jacksons lived in several small cabins on the property, where they entertained celebrities like President James Madison and Aaron Burr. The central portion of what was to become the Hermitage was constructed between 1818 and 1819 on a spot chosen by Rachel. The brick Federal-style house had four rooms on each of the two floors and two center halls. During Jackson's terms as president, architect David Morse added an east wing and a west wing, along with a front portico. In 1834, the Hermitage was so heavily damaged by a chimney fire—only the foundation and the exterior walls remained intact—that architects Joseph Reiff and William C. Howe rebuilt the mansion on the foundation of the original house, basing their design on Asher Benjamin's *Design Book of New England.* Six two-story columns were built on the front entrance façade. The most outstanding feature of the interior is the seemingly unsupported staircase. Classical set pieces replaced the furniture lost in the fire. The new mansion was completed in 1837. That same year, Jackson returned to the Hermitage after serving as president from March 4, 1829, to March 4, 1837. Jackson lived in the new Hermitage until his death on June 8, 1845. He and Rachel were buried in a tomb on the southeast corner of the Hermitage Garden. In

Rebuilt in 1834, the Hermitage is believed by many to be haunted by the ghost of Andrew Jackson. *Wikimedia Commons.*

1889, the Ladies' Hermitage Foundation purchased the Hermitage. Three years later, part of the estate became the Confederate Soldiers' Home, a residential facility for veterans. Before the home closed in 1933, the bodies of approximately 480 veterans were buried in a cemetery on the grounds.

The possibility that the Hermitage might be haunted was raised soon after the Ladies' Hermitage Association took over the old mansion. The story goes that two of the ladies decided to spend the night inside the mansion to protect it from vandalism. They had not been asleep for very long before they were awakened by moans and the clanking sound of a chain being dragged across the floor. A short while later, the house was shaken to its very foundation by a crashing, booming sound. Afterward, one of the ladies described it as sounding like a horse racing through the house. The source of the sound was never found.

The ghost stories persisted well into the twentieth century after the Hermitage became a house museum. An employee was locking up one night when he heard someone whistling. Thinking that his boss might have shown up unannounced to check up on him, he followed the whistling to its source, but no one was there.

Ghosts seem to be active outside of the Hermitage as well. People say that Jackson's ghost still opens the gate and visits Rachel's grave, just as he did when he was alive. Visitors and employees have smelled cigar smoke around her grave, as well. The apparitions of Civil War soldiers have been sighted walking around the grounds. Visitors frequently walk into cold spots as they stroll around the house. Many paranormal investigating groups believe that houses with as much history as the Hermitage are bound to be haunted.

THE HUNT-PHELAN HOUSE

Memphis

The Hunt-Phelan House was built for George Hubbard Wyatt in the Greek Revival/Federal style in 1830 at 533 Beale Street. Elijah Driver bought the mansion in 1845. The next owners of the house were Driver's daughter, Sarah Elizabeth, and her husband, Confederate colonel William Hunt. During the Civil War, both Federal and Confederate generals used the house as their headquarters. In fact, General Ulysses S. Grant is said to have planned the Battle of Vicksburg in the library. The mansion also served as a field hospital for more than nineteen thousand soldiers. Several presidents

The ghost of a faithful servant roams the grounds of the Hunt-Phelan House to make sure that the gold he buried there is still safe. *Wikimedia Commons.*

visited the house, including Martin Van Buren, Andrew Johnson and Grover Cleveland. Six generations of the Hunt family occupied the house until the mid-twentieth century, when a Standard Oil geologist named Stephen Rice Phelan acquired the mansion. In 1993, Bill Day, a member of the Phelan family, inherited the house from his uncle. While Day was restoring the house, he also discovered an impressive collection of Civil War–era letters from Jefferson Davis, Nathan Bedford Forrest and other important figures. Day converted the historic home into a museum, complete with family heirlooms, but he sold the house and its furnishings in 2000. Over the next few years, the Hunt-Phelan home became a bed-and-breakfast and a venue for weddings. In 2021, the property was for sale.

The most enduring legend connected to the Hunt-Phelan House took place during one of the darkest periods in the city's history: the yellow fever epidemic of 1873. Before the Hunt family took refuge in another city, a longtime family servant was instructed to bury a chest of gold for safekeeping in their absence. When the Hunts returned, they found his body in his room. They concluded from the mud and dirt caked on his boots that he had buried the gold before succumbing to yellow fever. An extensive search of the property produced no trace of the missing gold. Subsequent owners and occupants of the Hunt-Phelan House reported seeing a wispy apparition roaming around the grounds, supposedly making sure that the gold he buried is still safe.

Loretta Lynn's Haunted Ranch

Hurricane Mills

In 1965, country music star Loretta Lynn and her husband, Moody, purchased a beautiful antebellum plantation in Hurricane Mills. The property, which was known locally as Hurricane Forge, included Hurricane Mill, Hurricane Creek Dam, Hurricane Mills Bridge, the Hilman-Anderson House and the Hurricane Mills General Store and Post Office. Since then, the house where she raised her family has become a popular tourist attraction. In fact, she owned the entire town of Hurricane Mills. Each year, thousands of fans take tours of the historic home and museum to gain a window into the life of their favorite singer. However, some people visit the house in the hope of meeting the ghosts that have been a part of Loretta Lynn's family for decades.

The source of the hauntings in Loretta Lynn's house can be found in the past. While going through the historical record of the area, she learned that during the Civil War, a skirmish was fought on the property, and nineteen Confederate soldiers were buried there. This fact would account for her daughters' sightings of Confederate soldiers in the house when they were girls. Her oldest son, Ernest, walked into the "always chilly" Brown Room on the fourth floor and witnessed a soldier removing both of his boots. Her grandson, Anthony Brutto, told WJHL News that one night during a power outage, all of the lights in the house went out except for the chandelier. This would not have been an odd occurrence if the entire house had not been on the same breaker system.

The spirits of the former owners have also left an indelible impact on the property. Colonel James T. Anderson built the mansion in 1845. Despite the mansion's appearance, Anderson did not intend for it to serve as a plantation house. In fact, the metal columns were added in the 1930s to make the house look like an antebellum home. The spirits of James Anderson and his family have been sighted by Loretta Lynn and her family but by nobody else. Not

Built in 1845, singer Loretta Lynn's former home is haunted by several spirits, including the ghosts of Confederate soldiers. *Alan Brown.*

long after Loretta and her family moved in, she saw the door to the bedroom of her twin girls, Patsy and Peggy, open and close by itself while the girls were asleep. A few weeks later, the twins told their mom that they had seen a lady in a Victorian dress walk around their room. During a séance, an angry spirit who identified himself only as Anderson shattered the table. The spectral weeping woman Loretta Lynn saw in the graveyard and inside the home is probably the spirit of Beula Anderson. Following the death of her baby over one hundred years ago, she is believed to have died from grief.

After Loretta and her family settled into the house, she soon discovered that the scariest part of the house was a small cellar under the front porch. It was called "the slave pit" because in the antebellum era, unruly slaves were chained to the wall of the pit. Loretta said that one day in 1983, she and a friend of hers were watching television when they heard someone walking on the porch. Loretta opened the door, but no one was there. She sat down and continued watching the program. A few minutes later, she heard the rattling of chains coming from the slave pit. At that moment, she realized that the spirits of Civil War soldiers and Anderson family members were not the only ghosts in the house.

In 1984, Loretta Lynn and her family moved out of the old mansion and into a recently built house. Many fans assume that her song "This Haunted House" was inspired by the period when she and her family lived in Hurricane Mills because of lines like "I see your face before me every night / In this haunted house when I turn off the light." Actually, though, she wrote the song as a tribute to her friend Patsy Cline, who had died the year before in a plane crash.

Meriwether Lewis National Monument

Hohenwald

By 1809, Meriwether Lewis had accomplished more than most men do in an entire lifetime. Not only had he explored the West with George Rogers Clark, but he was also governor of the Louisiana Territory. Nevertheless, by the beginning of the nineteenth century, he had become a troubled man. In September 1809, he was on his way to Washington, D.C., to find out why his small expense account was not approved. Lewis floated down the Mississippi River on a flatboat to present-day Memphis. From there, he made the trip overland on horseback with the Indian agent Captain Maes Neely. At the time, Lewis was visibly ill, possibly from the combined effects of excessive alcohol consumption and stress. The pair had not ridden very far before two of the packhorses ran off with Lewis's papers in the saddlebags. While Captain Neely searched for the horses, Lewis continued alone.

Late in the afternoon of October 10, Lewis arrived at Grinder's stand near Hohenwald, Tennessee. That night, a couple of servants brought Lewis's buffalo robe and bearskin into the bedroom and spread them on the floor. Lewis preferred to sleep on the floor because the bed appeared to be infested with vermin. Mrs. Grinder recalled hearing Lewis pacing back and forth during the night and muttering to himself. After a while, he sat down in the doorway, smoking his pipe. Mrs. Grinder became so concerned about her famous guest's erratic behavior that she ordered her children to stay with her in the kitchen. Mrs. Grinder's fear prevented her from going to sleep. Suddenly, at midnight, she heard a gunshot, a mournful voice exclaiming, "Oh, Lord!" and another gunshot. Terrified, Mrs. Grinder bolted the kitchen door shut and refused to open it, even when Lewis begged her to. After a few minutes, Lewis staggered into the yard and began scraping the bottom of an empty water bucket with a gourd dipper.

Meriwether Lewis's restless ghost is said to be responsible for the spectral sounds visitors have heard around his monument. *Wikimedia Commons.*

The next morning, Mrs. Grinder sent a couple of her children to the barn where the servants were sleeping to summon them to the house. When Mrs. Grinder and the servants entered Lewis's bedroom, they were horrified by what they saw. Lewis was lying on the bed, with part of his head blown off and a large hole in his side. Miraculously, Lewis was still alive, but barely. In a strained voice, he begged one of his servants to put him out of his misery. According to another account, Mrs. Grinder heard Lewis say, "It's so hard to die!" just before he passed away shortly after sunrise. Around midmorning, Mr. Grinder returned from his hunt. He listened with rapt attention while his wife breathlessly recounted the last moments of Meriwether Lewis's life. Captain Neely arrived around the same time and heard the story. Immediately afterward, he sent a letter to President Thomas Jefferson, informing him that Lewis had committed suicide.

Mrs. Grinder's account of Lewis's demise is not the only one. Some historians say that Lewis's throat was cut; others believe he was shot in the back out in the yard. Robbery was suggested as a possible motive, because the gold Lewis was carrying with him was never found. Even Captain Neely was suggested by some historians as the culprit.

Lewis's body lay in an unmarked grave for years before being moved to the Meriwether Lewis National Monument grave site. The speculation surrounding Lewis's strange death is reflected in the historical marker at the grave site, which states that Lewis's life "came, tragically and mysteriously to its close." Lewis's unquiet spirit is rumored to be haunting his grave site and the memorial. Visitors report hearing the scraping of a gourd in an empty bucket and a spectral voice saying, "So hard to die."

NATIONAL ORNAMENTAL METAL MUSEUM

Memphis

When the U.S. Marine Hospital was built high on a bluff in 1884, south of downtown Memphis, it consisted of a stable, a laundry/dining room, a surgeon's house, two wards and the executive building. In 1936, a three-story brick Neoclassical building was constructed. The stable and the wards were razed in the 1930s; the surgeon's quarters were demolished in 1964. Only two of the original buildings from 1884—the executive building and the laundry/dining room—remain. They are listed on the National Register of Historic Places. In 1951, the name of the U.S. Marine Hospital was changed to the United States Public Service Hospital. In 1965, the hospital was closed. Five years later, the City of Memphis acquired the western side of the property from the federal government. In 1976, the City of Memphis leased the western side to the Ornamental Metal Museum. Three years later, the Ornamental Metal Museum opened its doors. The City of Memphis gave the museum a twenty-five-year renewable lease in 1992.

Stories of paranormal activity inside the National Ornamental Metal Museum surfaced soon after it opened its doors. Visitors and staff reported

The National Ornamental Museum occupies the site of the former U.S. Marine Hospital. *Alan Brown.*

Interns staying in the Artists' Residence have been awakened by spectral sounds in the middle of the night. *Alan Brown.*

seeing apparitions of soldiers walking across the grounds. The ghosts of nurses wearing uniforms from the 1880s have been sighted throughout the museum. One of the interns staying in the Artists' Residence claimed that every night around three and four o'clock in the morning, he was awakened by the sound of jars and bottles falling off the bathroom shelves. However, after the shelves were painted, the noises ceased. One of the most haunted buildings in the complex is the white building, which served as a center for yellow fever research in the late nineteenth century. Many people have reported seeing the specter of an elderly man in a wheelchair on the second floor. The apparitions of yellow fever victims have appeared in the basement, which served as a morgue during the epidemics.

The Memphis Paranormal Research Society has collected a great deal of ghostly evidence in the area where many of the victims of the city's yellow fever epidemics were buried. The members captured the image of a little girl in the morgue on film. They also experienced cold spots that dropped 30 degrees in parts of the museum, as well as orbs over three feet wide hovering over the ground.

THE ORPHEUM THEATRE

Memphis

In 1890, Memphis became home to the Grand Opera House, considered by many to be one of the most elegant theaters outside of New York City. After the Grand Opera House joined the Orpheum vaudeville circuit in 1907, it became known as the Orpheum. On October 16, 1923, a fire started in a women's clothier business on the third floor. The fire soon spread through the building, burning it to the ground. In 1927, architects C.W. and George L. Rapp undertook the construction of a theater with five floors, a fifth-floor gallery and seating for 2,800 people on the same site as the Grand Opera House. The $1.6 million project included the installation of a crystal chandelier and a mighty Wurlitzer organ. The "New Orpheum" was designed for live performances and for the viewing of silent movies. The Orpheum opened its doors in 1928, and it soon became the venue for some of the greatest performers of the day, including Duke Ellington, Eddie Cantor and Louis Armstrong. Over the next decade, the Orpheum's fortunes waned as vaudeville fell out of vogue. In 1940, the theater was converted into a first-run movie theater called the Malco. By the 1970s, the Orpheum—and downtown Memphis—had fallen into decline. In 1976, the Memphis Development Foundation was created to save the building from demolition. Soon thereafter, it was added to the National Register of Historic Places. In 1982, the Orpheum Theatre was completely renovated at a cost of $5 million. Improvements included upgrading the restrooms and the construction of concession areas. In 1996, the Orpheum stage was expanded to suit the needs of touring companies with larger, more elaborate sets. New technical equipment was installed, as well.

The Orpheum Theatre has been a showplace for live entertainment since 1928. *Wikimedia Commons.*

Like many old theaters, the Orpheum has a resident ghost. The Orpheum's ghost is the spirit of a twelve-year-old girl named Mary, who, in the standard version of the tale, was struck by a streetcar on Beale Street in 1921. Passersby and motorists carried her broken little body into the theater, where she died. In another version of the

The ghost of a little twelve-year-old girl killed by a car in front of the Orpheum Theatre has been seen sitting in seat C5 wearing a white dress. *Wikimedia Commons.*

story, Mary was one of the victims who perished in a fire in the original Orpheum in 1923. She is said to manifest herself in the form of poltergeist-like activity, such as doors that open and close on their own, disembodied footsteps and phantom voices. Mary's ghost seems to favor seat C5 on the mezzanine level. However, theatergoers and employees have also seen her running up and down the aisles. Sometimes, she announces her presence by playing a few notes on the organ. Eyewitnesses describe her as having long, braided brown hair. In most of the sightings, she wears an old-fashioned white dress and black stockings with no shoes.

A number of individuals have had startling encounters with Mary's ghost in the Orpheum Theatre. In their book *Haunted America*, authors Michael Norman and Beth Scott recount Mary's unnerving appearance in the theater in April 1970. Teresa Spoone was listening to Vincent Astor play the song "Never-Never Land" on the organ when she became very cold and goosebumps rose on her arms. When a ball of light flew into the last rows of seats, Spoone dashed into the lobby to see if the ball of light had appeared there as well. She received the confirmation she was looking for when several witnesses told her that they had just seen the ghostly figure of a little girl dancing in the lobby.

Mary also takes pleasure in interfering with live performances in the theater. For example, in 1979, a theatrical company from New York complained that their performances of *Fiddler on the Roof* were being interrupted by the manifestation of what seemed to be the apparition of a little girl with braids. After staff members told a few of the ghost stories about Mary, the performers held a séance on the balcony in an effort to persuade Marry to leave them alone. No one knows whether or not their séance was successful. When a production of *A Chorus Line* was presented in the theater a short time later, one of the actors who was singing off-key was joined by the voice of a little girl who seemed to be standing backstage. Unlike the actor, the little girl had perfect pitch. Her voice was heard a second time when the entire cast was standing offstage.

Mary's best-known appearance in the Orpheum occurred in 1982. Noted actor Yul Brynner was rehearsing for a production of *The King and I* when he was distracted by a little girl who was sitting in seat C5. He became aware that he was visited by a ghost when she suddenly vanished.

Not all of Mary's ghostly activity is mischievous. An organ restorer named Harlan Judkins was repairing the pipe organ late one night. He was all alone in the theater—or so he thought. After an hour or so, he decided to take a coffee break. When he returned to the organ, he was amazed to find that it was in working order. Judkins, who knew that the Orpheum had a haunted reputation, was convinced that Mary's ghost was involved somehow in fixing the organ.

The Read House Hotel

Chattanooga

In 1871, Dr. John T. Read and his son, Samuel, decided to build a luxury hotel on the site of the Old Crutchfield House Hotel, which caught fire and was razed four years before. The Read House, which opened on New Year's Day in 1872, was lavish indeed, with terrazzo floors inlaid with marble, carved and gilded woodwork and a lobby with ornate columns. On March 2, 1875, Chattanooga was devastated by a flood, during which a strong current flowed through the Read House. By 1926, the Read House was in decline. On the advice of two architects from the firm of Holabird and Roche, much of the hotel was demolished and rebuilt as a ten-floor, red-brick, Georgian-style hotel at the cost of over $210 million. The 237-room hotel includes the "Silver Ballroom." The Provident Life and Accident Insurance Company bought the Read House hotel in the mid-1960s. Today, the Radisson Hotel owns and operates the Read House Hotel, which is listed in the National Register of Historic Places.

The ghost of a woman who died in room 311 in 1927 still makes her presence known in the Read House Hotel. *Alan Brown.*

For years, guests have reported ghostly activity inside the Read House Hotel, such as bone-chilling breezes wafting through the rooms and apparitions. Guests staying on the fourth floor claim to have seen the ghosts of Civil War soldiers wandering through the halls. These could be the spirits who died in the original hotel back when the Old Crutchfield House served as a field hospital for the Union army in 1863.

Room 311 is said to be the most paranormally active room in the Read House. It is haunted by the spirit of Annalisa Netherly, who some say worked as a prostitute in the 1920s. According to legend, a jealous lover beheaded her in the bathtub in 1927, although some people believe that she might have committed suicide after her boyfriend abandoned her in the hotel and took up with other women. Guests say that they can feel her presence in the room when strange events occur, such as running water in the bathroom, flickering lights and unexplained noises. One guest complained that the toilet sounded like somebody was flushing it, but no one was in the bathroom at the time. Some staff members believe that Annalisa's restless spirit might be one of the shadow figures that appear inside the room on occasion. Her attachment to the room where she spent her final moments on earth might be due to the fact that many of the features from her time have been preserved inside the room, such as an AM radio, distressed hardwood floors and a claw-foot bathtub. The lock to the room still requires a physical key. The room was made available to be rented in 2019 following the hotel's $25 million renovation.

Roaring Fork Nature Trail

Gatlinburg

Roaring Fork Nature Trail is a beautiful 5.5-mile one-way loop through the Smoky Mountains. Tourists driving around the loop encounter old-growth forest, churning streams, old mills and other historic buildings, like Noah "Bud" Olg's nineteenth-century homestead. Some of the natural sites on the nature trail include Grotto Falls and Rainbow Falls, both of which are accessible on walking trails. The Roaring Fork Nature Trail is also the setting of one of the Smoky Mountains' scariest ghost stories.

In the year 1909, a horseman was riding past the Roaring Fork stream when he met up with a lovely young lady walking on the trail with no shoes, even though it was a chilly evening. Concerned for her welfare

The barefoot ghost of a girl named Lucy, who died in a cabin fire in 1909, can still be seen walking along the Roaring Fork Nature Trail, not far from where her cabin once stood. *Alan Brown.*

in this isolated spot, Foster asked the girl if she would like a ride home. Nodding her head, she introduced herself as "Lucy" and climbed on the horse's back. As the pair rode along, Lucy wrapped her arms around Foster's back. Due to Lucy's stunning beauty and the intimacy of the ride back to civilization, Foster fell madly in love with the girl. Within a short while, Foster dropped Lucy off at her home and vowed to see her again the next day. When the sun rose in the sky, Foster returned to Lucy's cabin. He knocked on the door, and when her middle-aged parents opened the door, he informed them that he was the one who had brought their daughter home. Then, holding his hat in his hands, he asked them for Lucy's hand in marriage. To his surprise, he learned that she had died two weeks earlier in a cabin fire. Over a century later, visitors driving and hiking around Roaring Fork Nature Trail have reported seeing the spectral figure of a young barefoot girl walking along the road.

Ruby Falls

Chattanooga

Leo Lambert, a chemist and amateur spelunker, moved to Chattanooga to pursue his hobby and to be with his fiancée, Ruby Eugenia Losey, whom he married in 1916. In 1920, he bought land at the top of Lookout Mountain. He then formed the Lookout Mountain Cave Company with the intention drilling an elevator shaft into the cave, the entrance of which had been sealed off in 1905 during the construction of a railway tunnel. In 1928, he had begun drilling his 400-foot elevator shaft through the limestone when he accidentally discovered a small crevice leading to another cave and its waterfall, both of which had been hidden. He decided to name the waterfall after his wife. He continued digging 1,120 feet until he found the original cave. He opened both caverns to the public in 1929, but he closed the lower cave in 1935 because it was not nearly as popular as Ruby Falls Cave. During the Great Depression, the Lookout Mountain Cave Company went bankrupt because of the decline in attendance. The new owners revived tourism in the cave by proclaiming "See Ruby Falls" on billboards and the roofs of barns hundreds of miles north and south of Chattanooga. A pathway around the basin was cut in 1954 to provide a better view of the falls. A secondary exit from the falls to the base of the mountain was cut in 1975.

In 1928, spelunker Leo Lambert discovered a subterranean waterfall, which he named after his wife, Ruby. *Alan Brown.*

By their nature, caves are viewed as spooky places, and Ruby Falls is no exception. On his website, Lewis Powell IV included excerpts from correspondence with Amy Petulla, coauthor with Jessica Penot of *Haunted Chattanooga*. Petulla said that the most active ghost seems to be the spirit of a security guard who fell down an elevator to his death in the 1970s: "They say that his spirit is

In 2014, paranormal investigators determined that Ruby Falls's entrance building and the caverns are haunted. *Alan Brown.*

accompanied by the smell of sugar cookies, which his wife used to pack in his lunch everyday." Petulla added that his ghost is credited with unscrewing the light bulb in a particular part of the cave, probably to let the staff know that he is still around. On September 6 and 7, 2014, Stones River Paranormal Society conducted an investigation of the entrance building and the caverns. Using video cameras and recordings of EVPs, the group communicated with the ghosts of Leo Lambert; his wife, Ruby; and the security guard who plummeted to his death in the elevator shaft. The members also made contact with the spirits by means of the "flashlight tactic," through which the ghosts respond to yes-or-no questions by turning a flashlight off and on. One of the members, John McKinney, was surprised to find evidence of the ghosts of children inside the lobby and the cave.

Ryman Auditorium

Nashville

On May 10, 1885, a magnetic evangelist named Sam Jones convinced Captain Thomas Green Ryman, a former riverboat man, that they should build a tabernacle. With donations from the people of Nashville, the Union Gospel Tabernacle opened its doors in 1892. Jones was scheduled to preach his first sermon in the church on May 30, 1892, but he failed to show up. In 1893, commencement exercises and lectures were held here. On October 25, 1894, John Philip Sousa's Peerless Band performed in the tabernacle. The Fisk Jubilee Singers put on a concert there on January 30, 1896. In 1897, a balcony was built to accommodate a large reunion of Confederate soldiers. Because many of the veterans contributed to the cost of the balcony, it was named the Confederate Gallery. A number of musical performances were held in the tabernacle in the early 1900s, including the Imperial Hand Bell Ringers and Edward Strauss and his Vienna Orchestra. A stage was built in 1901 for a performance of *Carmen*.

After Captain Ryman's death on December 23, 1904, Reverend Sam Jones took a vote during the funeral the next day to rename the tabernacle the Ryman Auditorium. Jones followed Ryman in death on October 15, 1906. Around this time, Susan B. Anthony, Booker T. Washington, Helen Hayes, former president Theodore Roosevelt and William Howard Taft gave speeches here. On July 31, 1915, firemen destroyed the stage to extinguish a fire that had started in the basement. In the 1920s and

The spirits of Patsy Cline and Hank Williams are two of the ghostly performers still making appearances at the Ryman Auditorium. *Wikimedia Commons.*

1930s, luminaries like Will Rogers, Ethel Barrymore, Marian Anderson, Helen Hayes, Katharine Hepburn and Tallulah Bankhead performed at the Ryman Auditorium.

The Grand Ole Opry was first broadcast from the Ryman Auditorium on June 5, 1943. Bill Monroe's Blue Grass Boys and Little Jimmy Dickens were some of the first acts to appear on the Grand Ole Opry. Mother Maybelle Carter and the Carter Sisters joined the Grand Ole Opry in 1950. By the end of the decade, country stars Jim Reeves and Johnny Cash were performing on the Opry stage. Patsy Cline, Charley Pride and Merle Haggard took the stage at the Ryman Auditorium in the 1960s. On October 13, 1969, the National Life Insurance Company announced plans to move the Grand Ole Opry to a new theater at Opryland USA. The Grand Ole Opry played its last show at the Ryman Auditorium on March 15, 1974. The Gaylord Entertainment Company purchased Ryman Auditorium in 1983 with plans to restore the venue to its former glory. On June 31, 1994, Garrison Keillor's *A Prairie Home Companion* was the opening act at the newly renovated Ryman Auditorium. In January 2012, the sixty-one-year-old stage was replaced with a new stage of medium-brown Brazilian teak. In 2018, *Architectural Digest* named the Ryman Auditorium the most iconic structure in Tennessee.

A number of different ghosts have been reported inside the Ryman Auditorium over the years. According to Ghostcitytours.com, the Gray Man, who wears a long, gray coat, is believed to be the spirit of one of the Confederate veterans who attended reunions at the Ryman. Not surprisingly, his ghost seems to favor the balcony, usually when the auditorium is nearly empty. A female spirit known as the Lady is believed to be the ghost of Patsy Cline. Her apparition has been sighted around closing time. Hank Williams's spirit manifests vocally. Employees at the Ryman have reported hearing him sing his songs onstage. Bill Anderson was playing one of Williams's songs during a sound check when midway through the song, the microphones went dead, and the lights cut out. No one knows if this was Williams's way of expressing his disapproval of Anderson's rendition of his music.

Possibly the most obtrusive ghost in the Ryman Auditorium is the spirit of Captain Ryman. As a born-again Christian, he seems to take offense at performances that he deems to be too risqué. Any kind of disruption during performances, such as curtains that close on their own or scenery that falls down, has been blamed on Captain Ryman's disapproving ghost. Sometimes, his ghost stomps his feet so loudly that audience members have demanded their money back. His antics practically brought a performance of the opera *Carmen* to a halt.

Making a personal connection to the glory days of country music is one of the main reasons why music lovers still flock to the Ryman Auditorium. Names of singers like Hank Williams, Johnny Cash and Patsy Cline are forever enshrined in the annals of the Grand Old Opry. At times, though, the past does seem to come alive in ways that are totally unexpected and, sometimes, alarming.

SENSABAUGH TUNNEL

Kingsport

Tales of haunted tunnels can be found throughout the southeast. Visitors to the unfinished Stumphouse Tunnel in Walhalla, South Carolina, claim that it resonates with the grunting and hammering of some of the 1,500 Irish miners who labored there. The ghosts of Confederate soldiers are said to wander through Tunnel Hill in Georgia. However, the most notorious of all the South's haunted tunnels is the Sensabaugh Tunnel in Kingsport, Tennessee.

Located on Sensabaugh Hollow Road, just off Big Elm Road, Sensabaugh Tunnel was built in the 1920s on land owned by Edward Sensabaugh. The eerie tunnel with a stream running through it has been rumored to be haunted since the 1960s. In the standard version of the ghost story, Sensabaugh was a farmer who lived not far from the tunnel. One day, he went mad, murdered his family and tossed their bodies in the tunnel's stream. In another version, Sensabaugh invited a homeless man inside his house, where the man received food and shelter. He repaid Sensabaugh's kindness by attempting to steal his wife's jewelry. When Sensabaugh caught the man stuffing the jewelry in his pockets, the panic-stricken thief snatched up Sensabaugh's infant daughter and ran out the front door. Later, the authorities informed Sensabaugh that they had found the little girl's corpse inside the tunnel. She was drowned.

According to an article published on Kingsporttn.gov, when Sensabaugh was an old man in the 1950s, he tried to discourage teenagers from partying in the tunnel by hiding inside just before sunset and waiting until a car pulled in. He would then scare them off by moaning and crying. Legends of Sensabaugh's antics morphed into ghost stories after his death in the late 1950s. Young people began spreading rumors that anyone bold enough to enter the tunnel at night would hear Sensabaugh's disembodied footsteps. They also said that drivers who parked their cars inside the tunnel and turned off the engine would be unable to turn it back on again. After a few years, the tunnel's ghost legends melded with the legend of the vanishing hitchhiker. Some locals swore that the apparition of a woman appeared in the backseat of their car when they drove through the tunnel. The identity of the ghostly passenger has never been determined.

Union Station Hotel

Nashville

Construction of Union Station began on August 1, 1898. On October 9, 1900, Union Station opened as a Gothic-style late Victorian building. It was designed by architect Richard Montfort (1854–1934) for the Louisville & Nashville Railroad. Its soaring towers and turrets were more reminiscent of a medieval castle than a twentieth-century railroad station. For over seventy years, the famous and the notorious paraded through the station, including

Mae West and Al Capone. To accommodate the thousands of troops who were shipped out from Union Station, the federal government chose it as the site of a USO canteen. By 1971, only one train—the Floridian—passed through Union Station. Two years later, the station's services were discontinued, and the building stood abandoned until 1986, when a group of investigators transformed the railroad station into a luxury hotel called the Union Station Hotel. However, because the investors used junk bond financing, the business venture went bankrupt. A second investment group bought the hotel and set about repurposing the train shed adjacent to the hotel. However, after the train shed was severely damaged by fire in 1996, it was razed four years later, and the investors decided to focus on an $11 million renovation of the Union Station Hotel in 2007. In 2012, the Union Station Hotel was renovated once again, this time a cost of $1.9 million. Two years later, Pebblebrook paid $50 for the old hotel, in addition to $15 million for renovations. The Union Station Hotel was designated as a National Historic Landmark in 1977.

The most haunted part of the Union Station Hotel is room 711. Legend has it that in the early 1940s, a twenty-year-old woman named Abigail arrived at Union Station to say goodbye to her soldier boyfriend before

Built in 1900, Union Station stood abandoned in 1979; in 1986, it was converted into the Union Station Hotel. *Wikimedia Commons.*

he was shipped off to France. They agreed that they would meet again in Union Station after the war ended. Following the signing of the peace treaties between the United States, Germany and France in 1945, Abigail returned to Union Station, hoping to see her lover climb down from the train steps and run across the station platform to embrace her. When she finally accepted the fact that he did not make it home from the fighting, she threw herself in front of an oncoming train instead of facing a life without him.

According to the website Ghostcitytours.com, after the war ended, a woman walked out on the train platform to have a smoke. Suddenly, the apparition of a young woman dressed in 1940s-era clothing hopped onto the rail and fell onto the railroad tracks. Still smoking, the woman was looking down at the tracks, looking for any sign of the young woman, when she saw a young man wearing a uniform from World War II standing on the tracks. She recalled that he appeared to be looking back and forth. Realizing that the scene she had witnessed was probably an episode from the station's past, the woman speculated that the soldier was looking for the young woman who ended it all when she could not find him.

For some unknown reason, Abigail's spirit prefers room 711 out of all the rooms in the Union Station Hotel. Guests have heard the phone ring and discovered that no one is on the line. Guests trying to get a good night's sleep have been awakened by the sound of someone moving furniture around in the room above them. Abigail's shadowy image has appeared in photographs taken in room 711. Folklorists say that Abigail's unfinished business—her rendezvous with her soldier boyfriend—is what is keeping her in the Union Station Hotel.

WHEATLANDS PLANTATION

Sevierville

In 1780, John Sevier's forces opened a huge section of the Great Indian Warpath on what is now State Highway 338 to pioneers following the defeat of a band of Cherokee warriors at the Battle of Boyd's Creek. One of the settlers who followed the trail into Boyd's Creek was a Revolutionary War veteran from Virginia named Timothy Chandler, who began farming on the site of the Cherokees' defeat at the Battle of Boyd's Creek. Following Chandler's death in 1819, his son, John Chandler, inherited the plantation.

A number of ghost stories have been generated by the Wheatlands Plantation's violent history. *Alan Brown.*

The farmhouse that his father had built burned down four years later, so John built a new plantation house on the same location. He called his plantation Wheatlands because wheat was the plantation's primary cash crop. By 1850, Chandler's 3,500-acre plantation was one of the largest in the entire South. At its peak, the plantation produced a wide variety of agricultural goods, including 150 pounds of wool, 200 pounds of butter and 200 gallons of honey. The plantation's distillery produced 6,000 gallons of whiskey. During the Civil War, the Federals commandeered Chandler's home for use as a prison. At war's end, Chandler began paying his servants a salary. In what would have been considered an extraordinary act of charity at the time, Chandler deeded the land along the south side of his planation to his former slaves. This community became known as Chandler's Gap. African Americans comprised the largest portion of the population of Chandler's Gap well into the twentieth century. Three entrepreneurs purchased Wheatlands in 2011. Their long-range plans included restoring the plantation to its antebellum splendor and establishing another distillery on the plantation grounds.

Ghosts from the property's tragic past seemed to have lingered on well into the twenty-first century. According to the website Blood Soaked Soil:

Haunted Wheatlands, seventy people died at Wheatlands, many of them through violent means. Twenty-eight Cherokee warriors who died at the Battle of Boyd's Creek are interred in a mass grave behind the plantation house. Fifty slaves were buried on the grounds, as well. Several women passed away inside the house. In 1888, one of the female residents of the house had a heart attack on the stairs and died. In 1932, another woman fell and broke her neck. Blanche McMahon, the last descendant of the Chandlers, died in the house in 1966. Bloodstains on the wooden floor of the parlor bear mute witness to a volatile argument between a father and son. In 1942, a man named Tim Johnson got drunk and began firing his gun inside the house. Terrified, his son, John, stabbed him to death in the parlor. In another version of the story, John stabbed Tim in the heart with a poker. Visitors have heard the thud of a body and unsettling gurgling noises in the parlor, leading experts in the paranormal to conclude that these are the residuals sounds of the murder that took place there so many years ago.

The ghosts of children have also made Wheatlands their forever home. People who have spent the night there say that the spirit of a little girl in a blue dress enjoys running up and down the stairs. The specters of slave children have been sighted playing in the yard. A little boy who was visiting Wheatlands with his mother said that he encountered the ghost of a little slave boy inside the house. He noticed that the boy was soaking wet. Suddenly, the ghost ran toward the boy, slamming into his chest and knocking him unconscious. The playful ghosts of children may be responsible for moving objects from one room to another during the night. Ghostly voices disturb the tranquility of the old house when no one else is around. Wheatlands is definitely an unquiet place, even when no one is around.

WOODRUFF-FONTAINE MANSION

Memphis

In 1845, Amos Woodruff and his brother decided to move to Memphis so that they could expand their carriage-making business, which was based in Rahway, New Jersey. After his brother returned to New Jersey, Amos explored several other business opportunities in Memphis, including two banks, an insurance company, a hotel, a railroad and a lumber company. In 1870, Amos purchased the Goyer House as a place where he and his family could live while work commenced on his dream home, a five-story French-

The vigilant ghost of Mollie Woodruff expresses her displeasure whenever changes are made in her former home. *Wikimedia Commons.*

Victorian mansion designed by master architect Edward Culliatt Jones from South Carolina. It had eighteen large rooms, three great halls and two tower lookouts. The house was located in the most upscale neighborhood in Memphis, appropriately called Millionaire's Row. Woodruff's magnificent $40,000 home was completed in 1871. Woodruff; his wife, Phoebe; and their four children—Sallie, Mollie, Cora and Frank—lived there until 1883, when they moved into the house owned by the Fontaine family. In 1892, Woodruff sold the house on Millionaire's Row to Noland Fontaine, who had come to Memphis from Raleigh in 1864. He and his wife, Virginia, had ten children. Fontaine made his fortune operating the Hill-Fontaine & Company cotton supply business. The Fontaine family became known for the luxurious parties they gave at their home. Their guests included governors and even the president of the United States, Grover Cleveland. Following an extensive restoration, the Woodruff-Fontaine mansion was opened to the public as a house museum in 1964.

The history of the Woodruff family proves the adage that "money isn't everything." Amos Woodruff's daughter Mollie lived in the house with her husband, Egbert. The promise of a happy, carefree life together came to a tragic end when Mollie's first baby died in the Rose Room shortly after birth. Not long thereafter, Mollie's husband, Egbert, died of a staph infection in the Rose Room. Mollie remarried and moved to a home on Poplar Avenue, where she lost a second child. Visitors and staff say that Mollie's mournful spirit has returned to the home on Millionaire's Row. Docents claim her wispy apparition takes shape whenever they try to move furniture. Her ghostly form has also been seen sitting on the bed in the Rose Room. If Molly's ghost disapproves of any decorations in the historic home, she slams doors and breaks objects. Everyone who has experienced Mollie Woodruff's spirit gets the feeling that it is still her house, even though she does not reside there in bodily form anymore.

Chapter 5

LEGENDARY WOMEN

THE BELL WITCH

Adams

America's most famous ghost story took place in Adams, Tennessee, between 1817 and 1821. In 1804, fifty-four-year-old John Bell moved his wife, Lucy, and their nine children from Halifax County, North Carolina, to a farm on one thousand acres on the Red River in Robertson County. John Bell's first encounter with the Bell Witch took place one day when he fired his rifle at a "dog-like" creature, which vanished instantly. Two of his children, Drewry and Betsy, also reported weird-looking beasts on the farm. John and the two children began hearing someone knocking on the door and window and the flapping of some sort of winged creature inside the house. Bell's children also complained of hearing rats gnawing on the bedposts. No rats were ever found. Sometimes, at night, their beds would begin shaking violently. The most terrifying disturbances were the sounds of someone choking and the rattling of chains. Only John Jr. and Lucy Bell, whom the spirit called "the most perfect woman living," were spared the wrath of the Bell Witch. She liked Lucy so much that she brought her fruit and sang hymns to her.

John Bell's family members were not the only ones on his farm who were harassed by the Bell Witch. One day, John Bell's favorite slave, Dean, was possum hunting in the woods with his dog. After treeing a possum, he cut off the end of the overhanging branch of a tree. Using his knife, he split the branch up about a foot. He then knocked the possum out of the tree, grabbed it and stuck its tail in the split he had made so that he would be able to hunt for more possums. All at once, he heard a spectral voice say, "This ain't no way to treat a possum!" Dean was then knocked down by an invisible presence and beaten on the head and body with his own axe. The next morning, Bell found Dean in his cabin. In a soft voice, Dean told his master what had happened. Dean bore the scar he had received on his forehead for the rest of his life. Afterward, Dean was attacked several times by a large black dog, sometimes with two heads, sometimes with no head at all. Dean swore that on one of his hunting trips, the Bell Witch turned him into a mule.

When word of the strange activity reached the ears of Andrew Jackson, he decided to visit the Bell farm. Jackson had formed a close bond with John Bell Jr. during the Battle of New Orleans, and he wanted to try to help the young man's family. He left Nashville with a party of men and a large wagon containing provisions and weapons. The wagon was pulled by four draft horses. The group had almost reached the Bell farm when one of the men cracked a joke about the Bell Witch. Suddenly, the wagon came to a dead halt. The driver cracked his whip over the heads of the horses, but the wheels refused to budge. Wiping his brow, Jackson exclaimed, "It's the Bell Witch!" A few seconds later, the men heard a booming voice coming from the trees: "They can go now. I will see you all later tonight!"

When Jackson and his men finally made it to the Bell farm, John Sr. threw a big dinner in Jackson's honor. That evening, while the men camped in the yard, Bell went inside the house for a drink. One of the men Jackson had brought with him was a self-proclaimed witch tamer. He accompanied Jackson into the house and bragged that if the witch had the courage to show up, he would defeat her with the silver bullet he kept in his pistol. A couple of minutes later, the young man jumped from his chair and began screaming that he'd been stabbed in his backside by a thousand pins. A few seconds later, his screams were drowned out by the booming voice of the Bell Witch. "I'm standing in front of you, witch tamer!" she shouted. "Go ahead and fire your pistol." Just as the man pulled his pistol, all of the dinner guests took cover. With trembling hands, the man took aim and fired at the space in front of him. The gunpowder ignited, and nothing but a little cloud of smoked belched from the barrel. Before the other men could start laughing, the witch tamer screamed that something was grabbing him by the nose and pulling him toward the door. When the door opened, the man was thrown out of the house. Then Kate proclaimed, "I will see the general tomorrow!"

Located on what was once John Bell's farm, the Bell Witch cave became the refuge of the Bell Witch after she ceased tormenting the Bell family. *Wikimedia Commons.*

Jackson's natural curiosity took over, and he told her that he would see her then. Fearing for their leader's safety, his men calmed him down and talked him into going back home to Nashville.

The Bell Witch enjoyed tormenting John Bell Sr. and Betsy Bell the most. The Witch was incensed with Betsy for her engagement to Joshua Gardner. Attacks from the witch became so severe that Betsy put off her marriage to Gardner. Over the next few weeks, she suffered from fainting spells and smothering sensations. The witch's abuse abated after Betsy married a schoolteacher named Richard Powell and moved to Mississippi.

The witch was especially cruel to John Bell Sr. Not only did she abuse him physically, but she also assailed him with threats and curses. After enduring this torment for several months, Bell was drained, physically and emotionally, and he became bedridden. On December 19, 1820, John Jr. took a medicine vial containing a dark, smoky liquid from the cupboard and gave it to his father. After Bell took the medicine, the voice of the Bell Witch began gloating over her defeat of John Bell: "It's useless for you to try to relieve Old Jack—I have got him this time!" John Bell died of poisoning the next day. The Bell Witch disrupted Bell's funeral by singing several bawdy drinking songs.

The search for the identity of the Bell Witch is complicated by her own conflicting statements. On one occasion, she said, "I am a Spirit. I once was very happy, but I have been disturbed and made unhappy." She also claimed to be "a Spirit from Everywhere, Heaven, Hell, the earth; am in the air, the houses, any place at any time; have been created millions of years ago." Many of Bell's neighbors believed that his tormentor was Kate Batts, the wife of Frederick Batts, whose brother, Benjamin Batts, argued with John Bell over the sale of a slave. Rumor has it that Kate created the Bell Witch to get even with John Bell. However, recent evidence suggests that Kate Bell probably had nothing to do with John Bell's "family troubles."

THE LADY IN WHITE OF THE GREENBRIER RESTAURANT

Gatlinburg

The ghost story connected to the Greenbrier Restaurant takes place in the late 1930s, when the building served as a lodge for hunters and wealthy guests as well. Most of the guests hailed from Memphis, Nashville and Knoxville, Tennessee. The story goes that a young woman named Lydia booked a room at the lodge the day before her wedding. The next day, the young woman dressed up in her wedding gown in the lodge and headed for the chapel. She walked into the church and waited for her fiancé to arrive. Several hours later, the jilted bride returned to the lodge. She threw the end of a rope over the rafters and hanged herself. Another variant of the tale also ends with the bride's hanging in the lodge. Making this version even more tragic is the revelation that her lover had been mauled by a cougar the night before the wedding. In one of the most fanciful variations, Lydia's vengeful spirit possessed the cougar, driving it to kill her lover.

According to mountain folklore, Lydia was buried in an unmarked grave because suicides were not given a Christian burial in consecrated ground. As a result, Lydia's restless spirit is doomed to roam around the site of her death for eternity. The story goes that the caretaker at the lodge erected a small cross on the poor girl's grave after being awakened several nights by a spectral voice pleading, "Mark my grave! Mark my grave!" After the caretaker erected a marker on her grave, Lydia's ghost never woke him up again.

A jilted bride who hanged herself from one of the rafters of the Greenbrier Restaurant has never really "checked out." *Alan Brown.*

Guests and employees at the restaurant say that Lydia's ghost is most commonly sighted on the stairs of the second-floor landing, where she is believed to have killed herself. Rachel Saults, general manager of the restaurant, told WATE 6 reporter Lexi Spivak that employees have heard what they described as a young woman's cries of love inside the restaurant. Saults said that a number of guests claimed to have seen Lydia's ghost. "I've even had some customers say they've seen a woman on the stairs, and I'll turn around and there's nobody there," Saults said. Eyewitnesses have described Lydia's apparition as being that of a petite girl. A medium who visited the restaurant informed Saults that Lydia's ghost "is not a fan of the beam" from which she hanged herself.

Lydia's ghost also seems to be partial to the kitchen. Workers say that cooking utensils placed in one spot at the end of the workday are found in an entirely different location the next morning. Food items have been known to fly off shelves, as well. Writer Steve Stockton believes that Lydia's spirit might be expressing her anger over a dessert item that is named after her: "Lydia's Chocolate Suicide for Two." The description of the dessert on the menu claims that it is "simply to die for."

According to Saults, the Greenbrier Restaurant is haunted by a couple of male specters as well. One of these is the ghost of a little boy. Customers claim to have sensed his presence under the bar. The ghost of an old man has been sighted in the back corner of the restaurant. "He's grumpy, and he doesn't like when it's loud," Saults said. The Greenbrier, it seems, is a happy place for the customers but not for its resident spirits.

MARY B. GREENE AND THE *DELTA QUEEN*

Chattanooga

The *Delta Queen* was operated as a steamboat on the Mississippi, Ohio and Tennessee Rivers for over seventy years. On February 11, 2009, it became a floating boutique hotel in Chattanooga. Aside from being recognized for its historical importance by the National Trust for Historic Preservation, the *Delta Queen* is valued by paranormal enthusiasts as one of the most haunted steamboats on in the country.

Mary Becker married steamboat captain Gordon Greene in 1892. She immediately set about learning how to handle their first ship, the *Henry K. Bedford*. Four years later, Mary received her papers making her an authorized pilot on the Ohio River. She assumed the role of captain after the couple acquired a second ship, although she refused to wear the captain's hat because it was "too mas-cu-leyne." She achieved nationwide fame when she beat her husband in a steamboat race from Pittsburg to Cincinnati.

After Gordon died in 1927, Mary took over the Greene Lines business with her two sons, Tom and Chris. Under her leadership, the Greene Lines' business interests included a cruise line. Business was booming, so Tom decided to add two boats to the line, the *Delta Queen* and the *Delta King*. Just one year earlier, the *Delta Queen* was being used by the War Shipping Administration. His mother loved their new acquisition, which had a special cabin, room 109, refurbished just for her. Unfortunately, she was able to enjoy the steamboat for only a year before dying in room 109 on April 23, 1949. She was eighty years old.

The first indication that a paranormal presence might be aboard the *Delta Queen* occurred not long after Mary's son Tom built the Mark Twain Saloon on the ship, despite the fact that his mother was a teetotaler. Just a few days after the saloon opened its doors, a small tugboat, the *Mary B.*, struck the bulkhead where the Mark Twain Saloon was located.

Seen here passing under the Market Street Bridge in Chattanooga, the *Delta Queen* was once piloted by Mary Greene. *Wikimedia Commons.*

The captain of the *Delta Queen*, Mike Williams, had a providential encounter with Mary Greene's ghost one night in 1984 when he was alone in the ship. Sometime after midnight, he was awakened by someone whispering in his ear. Unable to get to sleep, Williams decided to walk about the boat. Suddenly, he heard the door to the engine room slam. He ran down to the lower level of the boat, where he found water flowing through a hole. The ship would surely have sunk had Williams not been awakened during the night.

Mary Greene's next appearance aboard the ship changed Williams's life completely. One night, the new purser, Myra Frugere, informed Williams that an elderly lady called her up to complain that she was feeling very cold. Williams offered to go to the stateroom to check on the lady, but when he opened the door, no one was there. He returned to the room where he had left Frugere and was surprised to find that she was crying. After she settled down, she told him that she had been frightened by the face of an old lady staring at her through the window. Williams and Frugere were walking along the deck when Frugere abruptly stopped at the painting of Mary Greene and exclaimed, "That's her! That's the lady I saw." That night, Mary Greene's matchmaking skills undoubtedly came into play, because Williams and the young lady were married shortly thereafter.

TALL BETSY

Cleveland

The original legend of Tall Betsy dates back the late nineteenth century. In fact, the first reference to Tall Betsy in the *Cleveland Herald* was made in 1892. The story goes that more than one hundred years ago, Tall Betsy was a 7-foot, 6.5-inch woman who wandered around the streets of Cleveland at night, dressed in black from head to toe. No one knows the backstory of Tall Betsy. Some say that she was a police officer who dressed in black to scare curfew breakers off the streets. Others believe that Tall Betsy roamed the streets late at night to avoid the stares of passersby. She was said to have used a persimmon tree as a cane. Back in the 1930s, residents of Cleveland recalled that parents warned their children that Tall Betsy would take them to her mausoleum in Fort Hill Cemetery, eat them and gnaw their bones if they trick-or-treated too late on Halloween night.

Local businessman and philanthropist Allan Jones revived the legend of Tall Betsy on October 31, 1980, when he wore a black wig, a witch's mask and a long, black gown and handed out candy from his front porch. He claimed to have learned the legend from his mother, who had heard it from her mother. Children were terrified of Jones's house at first, but over time, they looked forward to seeing her. Eventually, the appearance of Tall Betsy every Halloween was turned into a huge block party, attracting hundreds of people. The event became so huge that celebrities like Little Richard showed up. In 1998, Jones decided to hang up his stilts and robe after twenty-five thousand people came to Cleveland for the festival. In 2005, Jones made his final appearance as Tall Betsy to mark the twenty-fifth anniversary of the first time she began handing out candy on Jones's front porch. On May 24, 1989, the Tennessee legislature proclaimed Tall Betsy as "the official Halloween goblin of Bradley County."

Chapter 6

LEGENDARY LOST TREASURE

THE LOST CONFEDERATE PAYROLL

Bradley County

Treasure hunting and history often go hand in hand. One of the most important historical events in southern history—the Civil War—spawned a number of well-known stories about Confederate gold, the most famous of which is the story of the lost Confederate treasury, which is believed to have disappeared in Wilkes County, Georgia, in 1865. Less well known, but equally compelling, is the legend of the lost Confederate payroll in Tasso, Tennessee.

Located in northeast Bradley County, Tasso has had a variety of different names over the years, including Fish Town, McMillan Station and Chatata (the Cherokee word for "clear water"). In 1905, the town was named Tasso after an Italian poet who made several visits to the little town. According to author W.C. James (*Buried Treasure of the Appalachians*), several Confederate soldiers from Company C had set up camp along the railroad south of Tasso in the spring of 1864 when the commander was informed that a Confederate train was chasing a Union train transporting two thousand soldiers. The soldiers of Company C were instructed to set up explosives along the railroad track just south of town and then detonate them as the Union train passed by. The Confederates did as they were told, but when they tried to blow up the Union train, the explosives failed to detonate until a few seconds later, completely destroying the pursuing Confederate train. A contingent of Confederate soldiers who had been watching from a nearby hill attempted to come to their comrades' aid, but they were repelled by gunfire from the Union army.

The loss of the Confederate train was devastating, not just because of the large number of soldiers who were killed but also because the Confederate payroll was lost in the explosion. According to legend, gold and silver coins were reportedly scattered hundreds of yards over a nearby field. In 1970, sixteen-year-old Ben Casteel found a rusty Confederate saber in Chatata Creek. In the next few weeks, searchers discovered belt buckles, parts of boots, mess kits, silverware and buckles around the creek. However, none of the coins that made up the payroll have ever turned up. Jameson believes that the coins, if they exist, are probably buried under as much as four feet of silt that has been deposited in the area by flooding over the years.

The Lost Spanish Gold of Elk River

Pelham

Legends of lost Spanish gold have fueled the imaginations of treasure hunters for generations, especially in the American Southwest. A good example is Montezuma's treasure, which, according to legend, is buried either in the Casa Grande ruins in Arizona or in other parts of the southwestern United States and Mexico. However, Tennessee has its own story of Spanish gold. In his book *Buried Treasures of the Appalachians*, author W.C. Jameson writes of a cache of Spanish treasure buried above the Elk River in present-day Burrough's Cover. The tale begins in 1886 when an elderly Cherokee man walked through the little town of Pelham. The disheveled stranger, dressed in ragged clothes and worn-out shoes, claimed to have walked all the way from a Cherokee reservation in Oklahoma. He spent the next two weeks knocking on doors in search of work in exchange for food and shelter. Just before he left town, the Cherokee regaled his listeners with a tale he had heard from the elders of his tribe about the members of a Spanish mule train who were massacred by a band of Cherokee braves three hundred years before. The Indians went through the sacks tied to the backs of the mules and found a hoard of gold coins and ingots. The warriors hid the Spanish treasure in a cave with the intention of using it later to make ornaments. This particular cave was distinguished from the others in the area by a cross carved in the rock cliff near the entrance and by a stream flowing out of it.

As the Indian walked out of town, he was followed by one of the residents of Pelham into the mountains, but he lost the trail. A few days later, the old Cherokee showed up in town once again. He explained that he had searched for the cave above the Elk River but with no success. After he left town to resume his search for the cave, he was never heard from again. In 1893, a group of treasure hunters found a weathered cross carved into a large boulder but no trace of the gold.

One theory regarding the mystery of the lost Spanish gold is that rocks loosened by an earthquake might have tumbled down the mountainside and covered the entrance of the cave. Another possibility is that the entrance could have been concealed over time by the undergrowth. Until tangible evidence is found, the lost Spanish treasure belongs to the realm of legend.

Perry Shults's Lost Mine

Grundy County

One of the Smoky Mountains' most enduring legends is the tale of the Lost Shults Mine. Perry Shults was a blacksmith who discovered a gold streak glistening on the ground in upper Greenbrier Cove near Webb Creek in 1867. Soon thereafter, the State of Tennessee granted Shults a ninety-nine-year lease on the nearby Porter's Creek to mine for lead, copper, zinc and gold. Every day, Shults and his wife took a different route from their home to the mine. Some people said that Shults entered the mine through a lengthy tunnel leading from Porter's Flat in Tennessee. While Shults worked in the mine, Mrs. Shults waited for him on a large rock. Shults was believed to have used coin reproduction plates to mint counterfeit gold and silver coins, his version of the U.S. Mint. When federal agents began combing the hills around Shults's mine, he reportedly threw the plates in the Pigeon River. He and his wife then packed up and moved westward without leaving a map behind them. Rumor has it that Shults buried a cache of his coins but never revealed its location.

The location of Shults's mine has tantalized treasure hunters for generations. A man who the bought the Shultses' home in 1967 uncovered a clay pot containing $37,000 while digging in the garden. A number of fake maps to the lost mine turned up in the 1970s, perpetuating the legend of the lost mine for decades to come.

Chapter 7

MYSTERIES FROM THE SKIES

The Great Snake Shower

Memphis

An article published in the February 1985 issue of *FATE* magazine featured a story about a strange "fall" from the Memphis skies on the afternoon of January 15, 1877, during a big storm. According to an article published in a local newspaper, the *Weekly Public Ledger*, thousands of garter snakes between twelve and eighteen inches long fell from the sky. After fifteen minutes, the "snake storm was over." Residents of Memphis reported that their gutters, yards, sidewalks and streets were completely glutted with snakes. The writer of the article noted that the creatures ranged in color from black to brown and that they tended to clump together. He also said that their color lightened when the snakes were immersed in fresh water. Local scientists collected several specimens and transported them to a herpetologist in Washington, D.C., who said that they were about the width of a knitting needle, not nearly wide enough for garter snakes. He also said that they did not slither like most snakes do. Instead, the reptiles "shoved the front part of their body forward and drew the balance up in a hoop shape," like worms do. The story ended with the statement, "Although the 'snake shower' was probably a far less wondrous event than it seemed, chances are we'll continue to read about it in books recounting great world mysteries."

On January 15, 1877, hundreds of snakes fell from the skies over Memphis. *Wikimedia Commons.*

A number of different explanations for the snake fall have been proposed for the "Great Snake Fall." An article published in the *New York Herald* speculated that a brisk gale had swept up a colony of worms and deposited them in Memphis, along with some rain. A few scientists have suggested that the creatures could have been common leeches or horsehair worms. However, the strangest part of this strange story is that nobody seems to have actually seen the snakes fall from the sky.

Tennessee's 1973 UFO Sightings

Middle Tennessee

In the fall of 1973, the United States experienced one of the largest waves of UFO sightings in its entire history. Owing to the large number of newspaper accounts of strange objects in the sky, September and October became known as an "Autumn of Aliens." A number of these unwanted visitations took place in Middle Tennessee. On September 3, a housewife and her three children saw a red triangular spacecraft with three white lights soar across the night sky above their South Memphis home. She reported the sighting to the Memphis Police Department but was told that the strange lights were outside of their jurisdiction.

On September 25, deputies from Shelby County witnessed some sort of object with two bright white lights floating above the ground in Memphis. A few days later, sheriffs in Obion and Lauderdale Counties claimed to have seen similar objects hovering over the ground. On October 1, three teenage boys told the authorities that they saw an egg-shaped craft of some sort not far from Anthony Hill. Inside the ship was a large, hairy creature that seemed to walk very stiffly.

The first week of October, during which two dock workers were allegedly abducted aboard an alien spacecraft in Pascagoula, Mississippi, initiated a rash of UFO sightings in Tennessee. On October 15, a family living in Berea reported seeing weird lights flitting around the woods near their home; around the same time, another witness saw what he described as a humanoid being with a glowing white head lope across the highway. Later, clawlike marks were found on the ground in the woods and along the highway where the sightings had taken place.

On October 17, sightings from Columbia, Hartsville, Knoxville, Lawrenceburg, Lebanon and Mt. Juliet were published in the *Nashville Banner*. Several separate UFO sightings took place in Middle Tennessee on October 18. A driver reported seeing a flying object hovering over his moving car near Springfield. In Clarksville, saucer-shaped objects and glowing cones were sighted. A farmer from Putnam County was in his field when two glowing lights zoomed toward him. He was certain he was going to die until, all at once, the lights flew vertically up into the sky. That evening, sightings of a silver cigar-shaped craft and several glowing objects were reported in the *Tennessean*, as well as a glowing blue mist that emitted whistling and humming sounds. In a sense, this was the grand finale, because no more UFOs were sighted in Middle Tennessee for the remainder of the year.

Where Did All the Dead Birds Come From?

Spring Hill

On February 28, 2015, the residents of Spring Hill found approximately one hundred dead birds on Northfield Lane. One of the eyewitnesses, Russell Thomas, was delivering pizzas at three thirty in the afternoon when dozens of birds crashed into the windshield of his white compact. Thomas got out of his car to remove the dead birds from his new car and then continued with his deliveries. Before long, rumors regarding the reasons for the mass deaths spread through Maury County. Suggested causes ranged from chemicals to a coronavirus. The Tennessee Wildlife Resource Agency collected several of the dead birds and brought them to the lab, where researchers noted that the birds were "split open" in a way that they had never seen before.

Scientists say that large "falls" of birds are not uncommon. Cold fronts and sudden rainstorms have been known to kill large numbers of birds. Avian disease has weakened flocks of birds, aggravating the stress of flight to the point that they die. Birds have also been known to die after eating large amounts of fermented berries. In their article "A Summary and Comparison of Bird Mortality from Anthropogenic Causes with an Emphasis on Collisions," authors Wallace P. Erickson, Gregory D. John and David P. Young Jr. estimate that man-made sources are responsible for between five hundred million to possibly over one billion bird deaths annually. Collisions with turbines, communication towers, power lines and buildings and windows also kill large numbers of birds. However, in the case of the Spring Hill bird fall, no conclusive cause has yet been discovered. Even loud "booming" sounds have been blamed for shocking birds. Yet in the case of the Spring Hill bird falls, no definite cause has yet been determined.

Chapter 8

MYSTERIOUS DISAPPEARANCES

David Lang: Now You See Him, Now You Don't

Sumner County

On September 23, 1880, David Lang was crossing his field, just as he had hundreds of time before. His wife and two children were watching him from the house. At the same time, Lang's brother-in-law and a lawyer were riding toward the house in a horse-drawn buggy. Suddenly, Lang vanished. There were no trees, no large boulders, no logs, no objects of any sort that he could have hidden or fallen behind. An inspection of the location afterward revealed no holes or abandoned wells or bogs that he could have fallen into. A geological survey showed no caves or sinkholes. For weeks, searchers combed the farm with bloodhounds, but nothing turned up. David Lang was gone, just gone, and no one knew why.

In the days that followed, the most compelling evidence was found by Lang's children. One day, they walked over to the exact spot where he had vanished and discovered a circle of stunted grass fifteen feet in diameter. His eleven-year-old daughter, Sarah Emma, called her father's name; immediately, they heard the faint sound of his voice pleading for help. The voice faded away in just a few moments. Excited by their discovery, the children ran all the way home and told their mother. David's wife visited the spot several times, and each time, the sound of the voice became fainter and fainter before fading away forever.

The strange story of David Lang received national attention after its publication in the 1953 issue of *Fate Magazine* under the title "How Lost Was My Father?" The article was purported to be the transcript of an interview given by David Lang's daughter, Sarah, in 1941. The interviewer was listed as Stuart Palmer. The article generated a number of fantastic theories regarding the fate of David Lang. Some people said that he was abducted by aliens and transported to another dimension in a UFO. Others say that he entered another dimension.

A more plausible explanation was proposed by Tennessee librarian Harshel G. Payne. After finding no mention of the incident in the local newspapers of that year, he conducted more research and could find no proof that David Lang and his family existed. Payne then explored the rational possibility that the story was nothing more than a hoax. Before long, he learned about a traveling salesman named Joseph M. Mulholland who enjoyed fabricating fantastic stories and sending them to local newspapers under the pseudonym Orange Blossom. The possibility also exists that Mulholland plagiarized Ambrose Bierce's short story "The Difficulty in Crossing a Field," published in the *San Francisco Examiner* on October 14, 1888.

Dennis Martin: Lost in the Smokies

Great Smoky Mountains National Park

The disappearance of Dennis Martin is one of the most baffling missing persons cases in United States history. On Father's Day weekend 1969, Bill Martin took his father, Clyde, and his two sons, Doug (ten years old) and Dennis (six years old), on a weekend camping trip at the Great Smoky Mountains National Park. They planned to spend the first night of their trip at Spence Field, running east to west along the Great Smoky Ridge. After Bill and Clyde put away their gear, they sat back in camp chairs and watched David and Dennis play hide-and-seek with two boys from another camp. Dennis ran alone into the woods while Doug and the other two boys darted to the treeline. A few minutes later, Doug and his newfound friends—whose surname was also Martin—sneaked up to Bill and Clyde and jumped out of the woods in an attempt to scare them. Once everyone had stopped laughing, Bill asked Doug where Dennis was. Doug said he didn't know, and everyone began screaming Dennis's name. After an hour, Bill contacted the

The two-week search for six-year-old Dennis Martin in 1969 was the largest in the history of the Great Smoky Mountains National Park. *Wikimedia Commons.*

park rangers, who immediately joined in the search, which ended when a thunderstorm rolled in.

The search continued the next day with over fifty people, including members of the Sevier County Rescue Squad, the Blount County Rescue Squad and the Smoky Mountain Hiking Club. Dennis's mother, Violet, arrived on the scene, confident that they would find her little boy soon. Psychics from all over the country offered their assistance as well. The FBI investigated the possibility that Dennis could have been the victim of a kidnapping. The family offered a $5,000 reward. On the eighth day of the search, approximately 1,400 searchers gathered at the scene. By the time the search ended, two weeks after it started, it had become the largest of its kind in the history of the Great Smoky Mountains National Park. So many people had volunteered to join the search that they inadvertently trampled over evidence that might have helped them find Dennis.

A number of different explanations were offered for Dennis Martin's disappearance. Some park rangers suggested that he could have been attacked by a bear or feral pigs, because their food source was scarce at that time. Most researchers believed that the child fell down one of the ravines in the area. His father, however, concluded that his son was kidnapped. His belief was based on a statement provided by an eyewitness named Harold Key, who said he saw a shabbily dressed man with long hair running through the woods carrying a red object. Dennis Martin was wearing a red T-shirt on the day he disappeared. The little boy was never found.

In 1972, the National Association for Search and Rescue (NASAR) was formed in Utah, providing a conduit for exchanging information and evidence regarding missing persons cases. Methods for searching for missing persons in the woods greatly improved in the years that followed. Undoubtedly, the urgency behind making these advances was generated by high-profile cases like Dennis Martin's.

Where Is Marsilene Smith?

Murfreesboro

On December 6, 2007, sixty-nine-year-old Marsilene Smith decided to go Christmas shopping by herself. Before leaving the house at one thirty in the afternoon, she took her diabetes medicine, without which she could have become disoriented and gone into diabetic shock. At the time, Marsilene was wearing a long-sleeved beige T-shirt, a blue denim jacket, blue jeans, ankle boots and diamond rings on both hands. When she failed to return home, her husband, Glover Palmer Smith, contacted the police. He told them he was concerned because he was unable to reach her. He added that she had blonde hair and wore eyeglasses, but her most distinguishing facial feature was a dime-shaped birthmark on her forehead. The police put out a BOLO—"be on the lookout"—for Marsilene Smith. Approximately twenty-four hours later, her champagne-colored Lincoln Navigator was found in the Walmart parking lot on Rutherford Boulevard. The car was unlocked, and the door was wide open. The keys were in the ignition. The police then examined the security camera in the parking lot and discovered that at two thirty in the afternoon, a man parked the Lincoln Navigator in the Walmart parking lot. He then took a green girls' bicycle out of the car and rode off. District Attorney Trevor Lynch believed that the crime scene had been staged to make it look like Marsilene had been abducted. A few days later, authorities discovered the bicycle and the clothing in the video.

Convinced that foul play might have been involved in the woman's disappearance, the authorities processed the SUV for evidence. A press conference was held with the family members in the hope that the general public could provide clues as to Marsilene's whereabouts. Flyers were distributed, as well. Police searched a wide area with cadaver dogs but were unable to find Marsilene's body.

Then, in 2009, a Rutherford County grand jury charged Glover Smith with fabricating evidence. During his trial in 2010, eyewitnesses testified to seeing Smith drive the Lincoln Navigator into the Walmart parking lot. The jury found Smith guilty and sentenced him to one year in prison and six years' probation. Since the trial, Marsilene Smith was declared legally dead at her family's request.

Chapter 9

MYSTERIOUS MONSTERS

The Flintville Monster

Flintville

The first sighting of the bigfoot-like creature that has come to be known as the Flintville Monster took place in 1976. A frantic woman entered the police station and told the officers a story that defied belief. She said that a "giant hairy monster" had attacked her car. She claimed that the beast broke off the antenna and then jumped up and down on the roof of her car. After the local media reported the encounter, other people came forward with stories of their own.

On April 26, 1976, a local woman named Jennie Robertson said that her son Gary was playing outside not far from the house while she was working inside. Suddenly, she heard her son scream. As soon as she ran out the front door, her nostrils were assailed by a foul odor that she likened to the smell of "dead rats." Then she caught sight of a humanoid figure between seven and eight feet tall loping toward the house. She could tell that it was not a person because it was totally covered in hair. Just before the monster grabbed her little boy, she snatched him up in her arms and dashed inside the house. After locking the door, Robertson looked out of the window in time to see the beast disappear into the woods. Before long, a large number of policemen and local hunters were combing the woods on her property. They continued their search long after the sun had gone down. Before they

This illustration depicts the "giant hairy monster" that terrorized Flintville in 1976. *Ben Shadden.*

decided to call off the hunt for the night, someone—or something—threw rocks at them. The next morning, the men found strands of hair, mucus, blood and sixteen-inch footprints. Scientists were unable to identify the species of the beastly intruder.

Encounters with the monster continued into the 1980s. Early in the decade, a housewife told police that a "black, hairy creature" chased her into the house. After she locked herself in, the beast beat on the door. Around the same time, a plumber told authorities that the monster had smashed his windshield. In 1989, several teenagers told authorities that they saw a "large, manlike ape" creeping across a field. That same year, a local pastor reported that "something" smashed the windshield and broke the antenna on his car.

Reports of bigfoot activity in Flintville ceased in 1993. Naturally, locals are relieved that "things have settled down." Still, they are perplexed by the identity of the creature that terrified the little town. They also wonder what happened to the monster.

THE PIGMAN

Meeman-Shelby Forest, Germantown

Hybrid monsters are a staple in urban legends. Examples commonly found in the American Southeast include the Goatman (Kentucky and Mississippi) and the Bunnyman (West Virginia). Tennessee's version of the human/animal mishmash is the Pigman of the Meeman-Shelby Forest.

In the standard version of the legend, one of the men who was working at the Millington Ordinance Plant was horribly disfigured during an explosion at an underground powder and explosives production plant during World War II. Shunned by fellow employees and the citizens of Millington because of the pig-like appearance of his face, the man took vengeance on everyone he came into contact with. His favorite hunting ground for victims seemed to be a bridge known as Pigman Bridge in Millington. Years after his death, the man's spirit haunts the bridge, terrorizing anyone who gazes into his hideous face.

In a variant of the tale, the "Pigman" was actually an insane hermit who tried to frighten people away from his farm by cutting the heads off pigs and sticking the heads on posts around his property. Some people say that he also decapitated trespassers who were undeterred by the pigs' heads and stuck their heads on posts as well. As in the other story, the Pigman's ghost still haunts his property.

In still another version of the story, the Pigman was an animal trainer in a circus. During one of his performances, one of the pigs he was working on turned on him and killed him. People say that his restless spirt, wearing the head of one of his pigs, wanders the Meeman-Shelby Forest.

THE TENNESSEE RIVER MONSTER

Tennessee

Unlike short stories and novels, which spring from the creative imaginations of individuals, legends are produced by communities. As the tales are passed down from one person to the next, storytellers imbue them with their own personal touches. As a rule, these alterations take the form of minor details, such as the names of people or places. In rare cases, major changes are made in the narrative, like the legend of the Tennessee River Monster.

According to an article that appeared in the *Kayseean* on October 19, 2021, the first sighting of the monster took place in 1822. A farmer was fishing from the banks of the river when all of a sudden, a serpentine creature rose from the surface of the water. The farmer was so traumatized by the sight of the prehistoric-looking beast that he died from shock shortly thereafter. The farmer's strange encounter was corroborated in 1827 when a fisherman's canoe was nearly capsized by what he described as a huge, bluish-yellow snake. As the nineteenth century drew to a close, some people were saying that anyone unfortunate enough to catch sight of the monster was cursed. However, an equal number of people dismissed these fantastic tales as the products of overactive imaginations or too much moonshine.

By the 1950s, the Tennessee River Monster had morphed from a reptilian nightmare into an enormous catfish called Catzilla. In the earliest legend, a man was repairing a crack in the dam when he was interrupted by the

The "Catzilla" that may be lurking in the muddy depths of the Tennessee River is probably a smaller version of this statue of the World's Largest Catfish in Wahpeton, North Dakota. *Wikimedia Commons.*

sudden appearance of a monstrous catfish that he described as being the size of a Volkswagen Beetle. He estimated that it must have weighed as much as five hundred pounds. The man was so shaken by the experience that he never dived again. Verification of the existence of the legendary catfish was provided by newspaper accounts of a work crew who were underwater cleaning out the intake of a power plant when one of the men was sucked into the mouth of a huge catfish.

The blue catfish is the largest catfish in North America, the largest of which on record weighed 143 pounds. The largest catfish ever caught in Tennessee weighed 118 pounds. One wonders, though, if the old stories depicted the existence of an entirely different species. The promise of catching something even bigger has kept fishing guides on the river in business for many years.

Tennessee Wildman

McNairy County

According to legend, in the 1890s, a creature that defied classification was captured and put on display in a freak show. Billed as the Tennessee Wildman, it thrilled and terrified everyone who saw it until it finally escaped.

Since then, eyewitnesses have described it as being seven feet tall with dark red hair and blazing red eyes. Its scream, they said, "curdled the blood" of anyone who approached it. It also emitted a stomach-turning smell. The powerfully built beast is said to have the ability to run swiftly and silently toward or away from anyone who comes near. The Tennessee Wildman has an aggressive temperament, especially toward women. In most of the reported sightings, the Tennessee Wildman is described as being not quite human and not quite Sasquatch.

The last reported sighting was the early 2000s in Elizabethton. Paranormal investigator Robb Phillips and his cousin were hiking to Bee Cliffs one dark, rainy night when the woods became disturbingly silent. Suddenly, they heard the cracking of a twig, followed by an ear-piercing scream. Terrified, they ran off in different directions. From his hiding place, Phillips saw a "stout" creature about nine feet tall clinging to a tree about fifteen feet away. From his vantage point, Phillips could tell that it had red eyes; long, sharp claws; and a sickening odor, like that of the rotting corpse of an animal.

The White Bluff Screamer

White Bluff

Named after the White Bluff Iron Forge, the small town of White Bluff originated as a Union army encampment during the Civil War. In 1867, the town was platted in a hollow, surrounded by a large, wooded area. In 1920, a family of nine built a home in the middle of this idyllic setting. After a few days, they were awakened by bloodcurdling screams and wails coming from the forest. Urged on by his wife, the husband picked up his rifle and entered the forest. After a while, he realized that the volume of the cries and wails increased the farther he was from the house. When it occurred to him that he was actually surrounded by an entire pack of creatures, the man hurried back home. Panting loudly, he threw open the front door. What he saw haunted his nightmares for the rest of his life. Lying on the floor were the dismembered remains of his wife and children. In a variant of the legend, the man is approaching the house when he sees a woman enveloped in a white mist leaving the house.

In the article "Nightmare Fuel: The White Bluff Screamer," author D.J. Pitsiladis tells the tale of a deer hunter who strung up and field dressed a large buck he had shot that morning in the woods near his house. He caught the deer's innards in a washtub. When he was finished, he decided to take a break on the front porch. The man was sitting in a chair, strumming his guitar, when he noticed that the ambient sounds of animals and insects had ceased. Suddenly, his hunting dogs raced past the house toward the dog pen. The man rose from his seat and gazed in the direction of the pen. Standing in front of the pen was a creature around eight feet tall. Later, he recalled that the monster was covered in white, stringy hair and that it walked on hooves. The creature chased the dogs around before turning its attention to the hunter. The terrified man ran back to the porch and slammed the door shut. The hairy beast began clawing at the door, screaming all the while. Frustrated, the thing walked back and forth across the porch before picking up the gut-filled washtub and vanishing into the woods. After the sun had risen, the man exited his house and walked toward the dog pen. The roof had been nearly ripped off the house. When he returned to the house, he found his guitar lying on the ground near the porch. On the surface of the guitar was a strange, slimy substance. The washtub was lying in a cluster of trees. It had been licked completely clean.

Chapter 10

NATIVE AMERICAN LEGENDS

Black Bear Myths and Legends

Smoky Mountains

For generations, the Cherokee people have viewed the black bear as a spirit guide, an elder and an ally. Black bears also provided the Cherokees with food, clothing, bedding, bone tools, oil or grease and jewelry. Bear robes were worn in ceremonies and were viewed as a sign of bravery by Cherokee warriors and hunters. In fact, black bears were so important to the culture of the Cherokee people that they figured prominently in Cherokee folklore.

One of the black bear myths that was told to children explains how he lost his tail. During harvest time in the Smoky Mountains, the days were cool, and the nights were freezing cold. Fox was a trickster, and he knew how proud Black Bear was of his long, beautiful tail, so he decided to play a prank on him. One cool, crisp morning, Black Bear was taking a walk when he saw Fox sitting on top of a frozen pond with his hair hanging down into a hole he had cut in the ice. Black Bear went over to Fox and asked him what he was doing. "I'm catching lots of fish," Fox replied. "I am going to trade my catch with the people in the village for beautiful tortoiseshell combs so that I will be the most handsome male at the dance of the Harvest Moon. I am sure I will have enough fish to trade, because as everyone knows, I am the best fishermen in these parts—even better than you!" Black Bear took Fox up on his challenge. "You think you're so smart!

For generations, the black bear has been an essential component of Cherokee culture. *Wikimedia Commons.*

I'm sure I can catch more fish than you if I fish all day and all night." That being said, Black Bear walked over to the frozen pond and sat on the ice with his long, beautiful tail hanging in the hole. The day wore on, and as the sun slipped below the horizon, darkness enveloped the pond and the Black Bear sitting on top of it.

The next morning, Fox ran back to the pond, where he found Bear sitting on the ice. His tail was still hanging into the hole, which was frozen shut. "Wake up! Wake up! Rise and shine!" Fox shouted. Wiping the sleep from his eyes, Black Bear replied, "Good morning, Fox! I wasn't getting any bites yesterday afternoon, so I decided to take a nap. It looks like my tail is stuck in the ice." Feeling guilty about what he had done, Fox offered to help Black Bear get his tail out of the frozen pond. "I tell you what, Black Bear. I'll get a running start across the pond and push you and your tail out of the hole." Black Bear was skeptical, but he couldn't come up with a better plan, so he agreed to let Fox give it try. Fox backed up onto the ground and then ran as fast as he could toward Black Bear. As soon as his paws were on the ice, he began skidding in Black Bear's direction. Fox slammed into his friend so hard that he popped out of the icy pond. When Fox noticed that Black Bear's beautiful tail was gone, he began laughing uncontrollably. While Black Bear was shaking the dirt and leaves off his fur, he looked back and was horrified to find that his once beautiful tail was gone. "I'll get you for this!" he roared and began chasing Fox. And this is why a fox will run as fast he can whenever he catches a glimpse of a bear.

Another black bear legend concerns a Cherokee clan called the Ani Tsa'gu hi. One of the young boys of the tribe began walking into the woods for extended periods of time. Each time he returned, he appeared to be a little bit hairier. When the elders asked him where he had been going, the boy replied that he had been spending time with the black bears, learning their customs and sharing their food, which was much more abundant than the food he and the tribe were having to subsist on. He added that he expected to join the bears after he had completed his transformation. The boy told the elders that they could join the bears as well, but first, they had to undergo a period of fasting. Before long, the entire Ani Tsa'gu hi clan left the Cherokee and joined the bears. Some people believe that the black bears living in the Smoky Mountains are actually descendants of the Ani Tsa'gu hi clan.

Generations of Cherokee passed down stories of a mysterious lake high in the mountains. It was said that the lake possessed healing powers. Even animals were aware of the lake water's ability to heal their wounds. Injured black bears were known to have jumped into the lake. When they reached the opposite side, they were completely healed.

Stories about monstrous beasts, such as giant catfish and monstrous wolves, abound in the wild. The Cherokee had a legend about a giant bear called Nyah-gwaheh. His magic powers enabled him to turn the tables on anyone who hunted him. Many warriors claimed that they did not hunt the creature for very long before they became its prey. The story goes that many years ago, four brothers took off in pursuit of Nyah-gwaheh. They were accompanied by a little dog. Called Four Eyes because of the dark circles above its eyes, the dog was said to be the best tracker in the region. One of the brothers, who had a reputation for being fat and lazy, decided to take a break. He reached into his pemmican pouch and found a handful of squirming, white, worm-like things. At that moment, he took the stories he had heard about the beast's magical powers very seriously.

One day, the little dog picked up the bear's scent and took off in pursuit. The hunters could tell that Nyah-gwaheh was the largest bear they had ever seen when he emerged in a clearing. When the fat and lazy brother twisted his ankle and fell on the mountainside, two of his brothers tried to help him walk while the fourth brother continued chasing the bear with his little dog. When the bear became tired of being chased and turned on his pursuers, the fourth brother drove his spear through the animal's heart, killing him instantly.

At nightfall, the four brothers carved up the bear and roasted the meat over a campfire. They had just finished their meal, when all at once, the bones reassembled themselves, and the brothers began pursuing it up a trail into the sky. The Cherokees believe that every year, the hunters chased the bear and caught up with it in the fall, when Nyah-gwaheh's blood drips from the sky and tinges the color of the autumn leaves a bright red.

CHEROKEE CREATION STORY

Tennessee

In the beginning of creation, the world was covered in water, and all of the animals lived above it in a place in the sky called Galun'lati. When their home became too crowded, the animals wondered what lay beneath the water. His curiosity aroused, the Water Beetle dived to the bottom of the water and returned with mud. The mud began to grow and was connected to the sky with four cords. The mud became what is now known as the earth.

A flock of birds flew down to the earth, but they could not alight anywhere because the ground was soft. Then Great Buzzard was sent down from Galun'lati. He, too, soared over the earth, looking for a hard place to land. When he reached what is now Cherokee country, he became weary, and his wingtips touched the earth, making great furrows that became mountains. The animals were concerned that all of the earth would be covered in mountains, so they summoned him back to Galun'lati.

After the ground dried out, the animals came down, but it was too dark to see, so they arranged for the sun to move across the earth from east to west. However, the sun was so close to the ground that it burned everything in its path. The medicine men were called upon to raise the sun. They raised it seven handsbreadths before getting it to the correct height.

Another world exists beneath this one called the Underworld. One gains access to it by following the streams down to their source. It is exactly like this world except for the fact that the seasons are different. We know that the seasons are different because the streams are always warmer than the outside air in the winter and colder than the outside air in the summer. To get there, one must fast and then ask one of the Underworld people to serve as a guide.

Men came to earth after the plants and animals. Human life began with only one man and one woman. One day, the man struck the woman in the head with a fish, and a child fell from the sky. The human race multiplied and filled all of the earth. They came so rapidly that it appeared that there would be no more room on the earth for anything else.

Lover's Leap

Chattanooga

In a sense, Chattanooga's history and the tragic fate of the Cherokee people are intertwined. In downtown Chattanooga is a memorial called the Passage. This waterfall stairway recalls the Trail of Tears, which began in Chattanooga. During the forced relocation of the Cherokee, Muscogee, Seminole, Chickasaw and Choctaw Nations from their lands in the Southeast to the western territories, thousands of people died. The suffering of the Cherokee people is also memorialized at Lover's Leap but on a much smaller scale.

Like many mountainous rock formations across the United States, Lover's Leap in Chattanooga memorializes the tragic love affair between Native American lovers from different tribes. *Alan Brown.*

For decades, Rock City advertised on billboards and barns across the United States. A good example is this barn in Hillsboro. *Marilyn Brown.*

One of Rock City's most prominent attractions is Lover's Leap. A scenic overlook on top of Lookout Mountain, Lover's Leap is 1,700 feet above sea level. Behind the cliff is High Falls, a waterfall that empties into the pool below. Lover's Leap also goes by the name "the Seven States Court" because of its panoramic view of Tennessee, Georgia, Alabama, North Carolina, South Carolina, Virginia and Kentucky. The cliff's romantic name comes from the Cherokee legend about a Chickasaw brave named Sautee who fell in love with a lovely Cherokee woman named Nocoochee. The couple could not have chosen a worse time to become lovers, because the Chickasaw and Cherokee tribes were at war. Knowing that their union would never be accepted by either tribe, Sautee and Nocoochee decided to run off together. As they were trying to sneak out of Sautee's village, Sautee was captured. He was accused of committing treason and thrown off the mountaintop. Because life was not worth living without the love of her life, Nocoochee threw herself off the cliff.

Connestoga and Nocatula

Athens

The legend of Nocatula has all of the elements of the classic tragic romance: love, rivalry and death. In 1780, a band of Cherokees discovered an English officer who had been severely wounded in the Battle of King's Mountain. Because of the Cherokees' allegiance to the British, the hunting party carried the officer back to their village. The chief, Attakullakulla, brought the young soldier to his house, where Nocatula Coowena, his daughter, treated the young man's wounds. While the soldier was in her care, they soon fell in love. Not only did Nocatula's father approve of the union, but he even adopted the Englishman into his tribe and gave him the name Connestoga, which means "the Oak."

One day in the fall, Connestoga and the other men in the tribe went out in the woods to hunt game. Connestoga was tracking a deer when one of his rivals for Nocatula's affections sneaked up behind him and stabbed him in the back. Upon hearing the sad news, Nocatula hurried over the spot where her lover lay. With tears streaming down her cheeks, the distraught princess took her lover's skinning knife and thrust it into her chest.

Custom dictated that the couple would be buried together. In an attempt to perpetuate the memory of his daughter and her lover, the king placed a hackberry seed in Nocatula's hand and an acorn in Connestoga's hand. Before long, saplings sprung from the seeds. In 1857, Tennessee Wesleyan University was founded on the site of the Cherokee village. By the 1940s, the hackberry tree had become diseased; it finally died in 1945. Within a few weeks, its partner oak tree began losing its leaves and died shortly thereafter. To commemorate the ill-fated lovers' tragic tale, the administration planted two new trees close to the site of the former trees. A historical marker summarizing the legend was erected at the site in 1957.

Reelfoot Lake

Northwest Tennessee

Before the 1811–12 New Madrid earthquakes, the now-extinct Reel Foot River fed into the Mississippi. The earthquake is credited with blocking streams, enlarging existing bodies of water and stretching the boundaries

Reelfoot Lake was formed by the New Madrid Earthquakes in 1811 and 1812. *Wikimedia Commons.*

of a cypress swamp to create a large lake. Following the earthquake, an eyewitness named Eliza Bryan observed that a massive lake was formed on the opposite side of the Mississippi River. The abundance of wildlife soon attracted hunters from all over the area, including Davy Crockett. According to the historical marker at Reelfoot Lake, siltation has caused the lake to shrink from forty thousand acres to fourteen thousand acres.

The Chickasaw legend explains the origin of Reelfoot Lake in a much different way. In the early 1800s, the chief of a Chickasaw tribe had a son whose deformed foot caused him to adopt a reeling gait when he walked. Reelfoot, as he came to be known, took over as chief after his father died. None of the maidens in his tribe would marry him because of his deformity, so he traveled south to look for a bride. When he reached the village of the Cherokee chief Copiah, Reelfoot instantly fell in love with the chief's beautiful daughter, Laughing Eyes. Repelled by the thought of his daughter marrying such a disfigured creature, Copiah prayed to the Great Spirit, who informed Reelfoot that if he stole a maid from a neighboring tribe, the earth would tremble, and the waters of the rivers, streams and ponds would engulf his village. Blinded by his love for Laughing Eyes, Reelfoot ignored the Great Spirit's warning, kidnapped Laughing Eyes at the end of the summer and brought her to his village. Having heard about the Great

Spirit's threat, Laughing Eyes begged Reelfoot to return her to her home, but he refused. During the wedding ceremony, the Great Spirit stomped his massive foot, causing a tremendous earthquake. In response to the Great Spirit's anger, the Father of Waters flooded Reelfoot's village. When the earth ceased trembling, a huge lake occupied the place where the Chickasaw village once stood.

Spearfinger

Smoky Mountains

Spearfinger (U'tlunta) is a Cherokee shapeshifter known to haunt the mountains between North Carolina and Tennessee. Her name comes from her forefinger, which is a long blade of obsidian. In the Smoky Mountains, the creature has been known to roam Noland Creek Trail and Whiteside Mountain in search of children. In her natural form, Spearfinger's mouth is stained with the blood of the livers of children. Legend has it that Spearfinger located the villages of the Cherokee by following the fires they made in the autumn to burn brush. Although she could take any form she wanted, Spearfinger often took the shape of an old lady. After gaining entrance into the village, she made friends with little girls, offering to brush their hair. After the children fell asleep, she punctured the back of their necks with her obsidian finger. As a rule, Spearfinger waited until the children died a few days later and then ate their livers. After concealing the body, she took the form of her victims so that she could become part of their families and take their livers, too. Villagers could always tell she was nearby because of the song she sang as she passed through the mountains: "Liver, I eat it." Spearfinger was entirely made of stone. She could be killed only by stabbing her heart, which she protected in her clenched hand. Knowing that the Cherokee were distrustful of outsiders, Spearfinger often took the shape of other seemingly harmless beings, such as squirrels. For generations, parents warned their children that Spearfinger would "get them" if they wandered too far from the village at night.

Spearfinger's enemy was Stone Man, who was immensely strong, with the ability to lift rocks and boulders. Stone Man was feared by the Cherokee because he, too, had a fondness for the livers of children. To facilitate traveling from one mountain to the next, Stone Man built a great rock bridge. The story goes that Stone Man's eagerness to overstep his bounds angered the higher beings, who cast down thunderbolts and destroyed the bridge. Stone Man is believed to walk the hills along Norton Creek in the Great Smoky Mountains.

Stories of Spearfinger can be found throughout Cherokee folklore. In one of the most commonly told tales, the villagers became tired of losing their children to Spearfinger, so they devised a plan to get of rid of her once and for all. They dug a pit and then stuck several sharp stakes into the bottom. They then laid branches over the top for camouflage. To lure her into the village, they made large fires and began roasting chestnuts. Attracted by the smoke, Spearfinger transformed into an old woman and concealed the hand with the spearfinger under her cloak. Recognizing her, the men began firing arrows at her. As the arrows bounced off her stone hide and fell to the ground, Spearfinger was consumed by anger and charged the warriors. Suddenly, she crashed through the branches and fell into the hole. When the warriors ran over to the pit, a titmouse cried, "Heart! Heart! Heart!" Thinking that the creature's heart was in her chest, the men fired their arrows, but they had no effect. When a chickadee flew down from the sky and landed on Spearfinger's hand, she began shaking in fear. Taking the hint, the warriors shot her in the wrist, causing her to drop her heart. She would trouble the Cherokee no more.

Tlanuhwa and Uhktena

Tennessee

When the earth was new, the spirit beings lived in the Above World, and monstrous snakes, lizards and amphibians lived in the Below World. Sometimes, these giant creatures emerged from caves, lakes and rivers and visited the Middle World. The most terrifying of these monsters, the Uhktena, was a massive snake with wings on its back and horns on its head.

The Tlanuhwa were massive hawks with markings like today's red-tailed hawks. They made their nests in a cave on a rock cliff. While swooping over the rivers, they occasionally made off with dogs, cats and small children. Cherokee warriors fired arrows at the giant birds as they flew by, but the arrows merely glanced off their feathers. In desperation, the people asked a medicine man for help. He made a long rope out of vines and fashioned loops for his feet. The men lowered him down to the cave. He climbed inside and found four fledgling birds and several unhatched eggs. He also discovered that all of the children the Tlanuhwa had carried off were stored away inside. Suddenly, the Tlanuhwa returned with more children in their talons. To distract the birds, the medicine man grabbed the fledgling birds and the eggs and tossed them into the river, where they were devoured by the Uhktena. Enraged at the sight of their chicks being eaten, the Tlanuhwa dropped the children and flew down to do battle with the Uhktena. The children were caught by the men waiting at the bottom of the cliff. One of the Tlanuhwa grabbed the Uhktena and carried it up into the sky, and one of the others tore it into four pieces. The giant hawks flew higher and higher until they were completely out of sight. They were never seen again.

The Wampus Cat

Appalachian Trail

The Wampus Cat is said to be a large cat-like creature that prowls the hills and forests of Arkansas, Missouri, North Carolina, Southeastern Appalachia, and Tennessee. Since the early 1800s, residents in these areas have claimed that the two-legged beast has a catlike nose and face and that it walks on its hind legs. It is known for stealing pets and killing livestock.

The origin story of the Wampus Cat exists in at least two versions. According to the Anglo version, a beautiful Cherokee woman begged her husband to be allowed to observe the men's secret hunting rituals, but he refused. One day, her curiosity got the best of her. She wrapped herself up in a cougar skin and crept through the woods toward the spot where the men were seated in a circle around a campfire. She sat several feet away from the campfire until, all at once, she was grabbed from behind and dragged off. The shaman punished her by casting a spell that transformed her into a human-cougar hybrid. Shunned by cougars and human beings alike, she wanders through the woods alone, catching and eating whatever she can.

The Wampus Cat of Cherokee folklore is entirely different. Many years ago, an evil spirit called the Ew'ah—"the Spirit of Madness"—was ravaging a village called Etowah. Anyone unlucky enough to see the creature was instantly driven mad. In desperation, the shamans and elders decided to send one of the bravest men in the village—a warrior named Standing Bear—to destroy the demon. Equipped with the best weapons, Standing Bear kissed his wife, Running Deer, goodbye. When he returned several weeks later, he had lost his mind. Outraged that her husband was just a

Many people believe that the Wampus Cat is actually a misidentified cougar. *Wikimedia Commons.*

shadow of his former self, Running Deer asked the shamans if they would help her take revenge on the Ew'ah. Outfitted with a bobcat's face—a cat-spirit mask—and covered with a black paste to mask her scent, she walked into the forest in search of the creature. She made her way to the creek where her husband had been driven mad. In the mud not far from Standing Bear's breastplate were the prints of the demon. Running Deer followed the tracks until she found the demon crouched by the spring, drinking water. Without a moment's hesitation, Running Deer pounced on the Ew'ah. Author David Tabler says that with the aid of the cat-spirit mask, she "turned its powerful magic back on itself. The We'ah tumbled backwards into the pool, and Running Deer immediately turned on her heel and ran as fast as she could back to the village, never once looking back." The Cherokee believed that Running Deer became a spirit called the Home-Protector and lives on in the Wampus Cat.

Chapter 11

UNIVERSITY LEGENDS

Austin Peay State University

Clarksville

The institution that is now Austin Peay State University had its beginnings in the Montgomery Male Academy, which was founded in 1845. Three years later, it merged with the Masonic College and became the Montgomery Masonic College and Male Academy. In 1855, the Presbyterian Synod of Nashville acquired the school and changed the name to Stewart College. In 1862, the school was evacuated by Union soldiers who were marching from Fort Donelson to take Fort Defiance. A few years later, the name was changed to Southwestern Presbyterian University. In 1927, the school was moved to the Clarksville campus, and the name was changed to Austin Peay Normal School in honor of Governor Austin Peay. The name was changed once again in 1943, this time to Austin Peay State College. In 1951, the school was authorized to confer the bachelor of arts degree. The graduate school opened the next year, offering the degree of master of arts in education. In 1999, an F3 tornado ravaged downtown Clarksville. Three campus buildings—Harned, Harvill and Archwood—were severely damaged. Between 2001 and 2010, enrollment increased 52.4 percent. Enrollment surpassed the ten-thousand-student mark in 2009.

Harned Hall is one of the most haunted buildings on campus. Built in 1931, it was the first new building constructed during the Normal School

The original part of the Austin Peay Memorial Building was built in 1910 as the Carnegie Library. *Wikimedia Commons.*

era. It continued serving as a women's residence hall until the 1980s. Like many college dormitories, Harned Hall is said to be haunted by the ghost of a student who hanged herself, either from the second-story balcony or from the railings in the stairwell. Even though no record has been found indicating that anyone killed herself back when the building was a dormitory, tales of hauntings persist.

During its stay on campus in 1862, the Union army commandeered an old dormitory for use as a field hospital. This building is now the Felix G. Woodward Library. Psychic residue from that period in history has made the library one of the most haunted buildings on campus. Since the 1990s, students and librarians have reported hearing phantom voices and other unnerving sounds. In 2009, paranormal investigator Lorraine Warren reported that when she walked through the basement of the library, she had a vision of hospital cots lined up against the walls, just as they would have been during the Civil War.

By their very nature, all ghosts are unusual, but strangest by far is the spirit that is haunting the Memorial Health Building/Red Barn. For years, the Red Barn was used for basketball games and concerts. In the 1940s, a farmer loaned his mule to the men who were constructing the Memorial Health Building. Small children loved riding the gentle animal in the Castle Heights neighborhood. When the mule finally died, it was buried in a field. A few years later, the Memorial Health Building was constructed over the site. Some people believe that the mule was buried under center court. The old mule is dead, but it is still there in spirit. The unmistakable sound of braying and the clopping of hooves inside the building seems to be the mule's way of announcing his presence.

The Trahern Building houses the Department of Art and Design and the Department of Theatre and Dance. According to campus lore, the building is haunted by the ghost of a woman named Margaret. Students and employees say that the third floor is the site of most of the paranormal activity. Margaret is a playful ghost who enjoys slamming doors, dropping props on the stage floor and making the orchestra lift get stuck. In 2002, Margaret was accused of making the lights go out during the rehearsal for a play. A student named Mylisha Edwards said that she was putting away type in the printing room when a girl came in and sat down. Ten minutes later, after finishing working in the printing room, Edwards checked on the girl. She was gone. People familiar with the history of the school have theorized that the spirit could be the ghost of Margaret Elwyn Trahern, the first woman to graduate from Austin Peay, or Margaret Fort Trahern, a longtime art instructor and patron of the arts. So far, the ghost's true identity has not been determined.

EASTERN TENNESSEE STATE UNIVERSITY

Johnson City

Eastern Tennessee State University started out as East Tennessee State Normal School when it opened its doors in 1911. The K–12 training school still operates to this day under the name University School. The school became East Tennessee State Teachers College in 1925. In 1927, the Normal School received accreditation from the Southern Association of Colleges and Secondary Schools. Three years later, the institution underwent a third name change as East Tennessee State Teachers College, Johnson City. After expanding its curriculum to include an expansive liberal arts curriculum in 1943, the school became East Tennessee State College. In 1963, the name was changed to East Tennessee State University (ETSU) to reflect its wide range of majors and minors. In 2005, plans were made to open a college of pharmacy. A doctoral program in sports physiology and performance—the first of its kind in the United States—was authorized in 2009. Today, East Tennessee State University offers over 140 academic programs.

Many students claim to have had paranormal experiences in Gilbreath Hall, which houses the College of Arts and the Science, Math and Foreign Languages Departments. They say the hall is haunted by the ghost of Sidney Gilbreath, the founder and former president of Eastern Tennessee State University. Uncle Sid, as students call him, is an authoritative spirit who tells students loitering in the halls to get to class. Students also say that he closes doors and windows and turns off lights carelessly left on. A female student said that one day, all of the computers in a class turned on at the same time, all by themselves. When the lab instructor jokingly blamed "Uncle Sid," the student suddenly felt a wave of cold wash over her, as if something cold had

This is the quad at East Tennessee State University, which opened its doors in 1911. *Wikimedia Commons.*

just walked by. Supposedly, the ghost's favorite part of the building is the top floor, which has been blocked off for many years.

Burleson Hall, the English building, is believed to be haunted by the ghost of a popular English professor named Christine Burleson. She taught Shakespeare for decades until she was afflicted by a debilitating disease. Confined to a wheelchair toward the end of her life, she died by suicide in the early 1970s. Students and staff have heard the moaning of a woman in Burleson Hall. Some students believe that the eyes in the portrait of Burleson's father, which hangs on one of the walls, follow them around. A few believe they are actually Christine Burleson's eyes.

Haunted libraries can be found in campuses across the United States, and ETSU is no exception. The four-story Charles C. Sherrod Library, which houses the Archives of Appalachia and University Archives, has sixty-two individual study rooms and fourteen group study rooms. According to Charles Edwin Price's book *More Haunted Tennessee*, Sherrod Library is haunted by the ghost of a former librarian who is believed to be a vigilant presence in the library. Students and employees browsing through the stacks have felt someone looking over their shoulder at them. A staff member told Price that she had just walked down the iron stairs to the lowest level of the library when she saw a ghostly figure going down the stairs. The specter had no arms or legs: "What I saw was the torso of a woman, dressed in an old-fashioned, high-neck maroon dress, gliding down the stairs. My blood turned to ice. I could see her clearly. She had a very stern expression and was wearing old-fashioned, wire-rimmed glasses. I couldn't move. Then the figure disappeared."

Lucille-Clements Hall is reputed to be the most haunted building on campus. One of the students living in the dormitory woke up one morning to find the ghost of Lucille Clements standing over her roommate's bed, staring down at her. She woke up her roommate to tell her what she saw; in a sleepy voice, her roommate said, "It's just Lucy. You know that!" and went back to sleep. Many students blame the ghosts of children for some of the poltergeist activity in the dorm, such as the faucets that seem to turn off and on by themselves, televisions that turn on by themselves and objects that fly through the air. Legend has it that one of these playful spirits is the apparition of a little boy who fell down an elevator shaft while playing a game of marbles. Many students claim to have heard marbles rolling around on the floor at night.

Lincoln Memorial University

Harrogate

In 1897, General O.O. Howard teamed up with Reverend Arthur A. Meyers and his wife to found a four-year institution of higher learning in the Cumberland Gap. Lincoln Memorial University was a dream come true for General Howard, who recalled a conversation he had with President Abraham Lincoln in 1863, in which Lincoln expressed his desire to thank the people of East Tennessee for their support during the war by doing something to help them. General Howard felt that founding the university fulfilled Lincoln's wish. Cyrus Kerr was appointed the university's first president. Howard and his friends donated their personal collection of Lincoln artifacts to the Abraham Lincoln Library and Museum. The museum now has one of the largest collections of Lincoln memorabilia in the United States.

General Howard chose a plot of land once occupied by a luxury hotel as the site of Lincoln Memorial University. The Four Seasons Hotel and Sanitorium was built in 1892. Its guests included luminaries like Cornelius

One of the exhibits at the Abraham Lincoln Library and Museum is a human jawbone once believed to be that of Abraham Lincoln. *Wikimedia Commons.*

Vanderbilt and Mark Twain. In 1904, the hotel burned down. Using blocks from the ruins of the sanitarium, the university constructed Grant-Lee Hall, the first dormitory, which is now on the National Register of Historic Places.

Grant-Lee Hall is reputed to be haunted by the ghost of a woman who died, along with her child, on the fourth floor in the fire of 1904. She was wearing a red dress at the time. When the building caught fire again in 1950, spectators saw a woman in a red dress on the fourth floor, screaming for help. For many years, students living in the residence hall have heard footsteps on the stairs. Phantom knocks on the doors are accompanied by the twisting of doorknobs. Could it be that the Woman in Red is trying to warn the residents of the fire that claimed her life?

Another campus legend concerns the Abraham Lincoln Library and Museum. Many students believe that Abraham Lincoln's ghost wanders the halls of the library in search of his missing jawbone. According to the university archivist, in 1912, a package containing a human jawbone was mailed to the university, along with a note explaining that it was Abraham Lincoln's jawbone and that it had been stolen by a group of fraternity boys. The jawbone now resides in the Abraham Lincoln Library and Museum, but it is not Lincoln's. No one knows who is the rightful owner of the mystery jawbone.

Middle Tennessee State University

Murfreesboro

Middle Tennessee State University opened as a teacher training school on September 11, 1911. It became a four-year teachers college in 1925. In 1943, its designation was changed to that of a state university. The school was designated a university in 1965. Over one hundred thousand students have graduated from Middle Tennessee University since 1911.

The Tucker Theatre was named for Dorothe "Dot" Tucker—the founder of the Department of Theatre and Dance at the university—and her husband, Dr. Clay Tucker, dean of the College of Liberal Arts, in 1987. The theater that bears their name is believed to be haunted by two ghosts. The first of these is the ghost of a former MTSU professor. In 2019, a lighting designer and his friend saw a seat lower by itself, just as if someone were trying to sit down. The pair also detected the odor of cigarette smoke in the auditorium. The second ghost is the spirit of a young woman who

The Homer Pittard Campus School is one of the oldest buildings on the campus of Middle Tennessee State University. *Wikimedia Commons.*

died in the auditorium. One night, when the lighting tech and a professor were working in the auditorium, both of them saw a young woman walk up the aisle.

The Boutwell Dramatic Arts Building is believed to be haunted as well. One day, the lighting tech and two other students were working on designs for a play in the Language Lab when one of them—the lighting tech—decided to close the door of the Language Lab and walk down the hallway. When the two students returned to the Language Lab, they were surprised to find the door open. They also realized that the third student—the lighting tech—was no longer with them. They walked inside the Language Lab and found the young man leaning against a far wall, crying uncontrollably. With tears streaming down his face, he told his friends to touch him. When they did, his skin felt very warm to the touch.

As the three students left the Language Lab, they heard footsteps walking toward the ladies' room. The female student walked into the bathroom and exited immediately. She said that one of the stall doors was locked. When she bent down, she saw a pair of legs ending at a pair of white tennis shoes. Wondering why anyone would be in there at two o'clock in the morning, the lighting tech walked inside and put his hand on the stall door. Closing his eyes, he got an impression of a college-age Asian woman with long, black hair and a red-and-white polka-dot dress sitting inside the stall. The three students left the building immediately. Two days later, the lighting tech was driving past the Boutwell Dramatic Arts Building late at night when he looked up and saw the same Asian woman staring out of one of the windows of the Language Lab.

Tennessee Wesleyan University

Athens

The institution that became Tennessee Wesleyan University originated in 1857 as Athens Female College. The name was changed early on, in 1866, to East Tennessee Wesleyan College and to East Tennessee Wesleyan University in 1867. To garner support from northern philanthropists, President John F. Spence changed the name to Grant Memorial University. Three years later, the school became U.S. Grant Memorial University when it merged with Chattanooga University. The university acquired the name Athens School of the University of Chattanooga in 1906. After splitting from Chattanooga in 1925, the school became a junior college named Tennessee Wesleyan College. When the institution began offering bachelor's degrees in 1957, it became a liberal arts college. On July 1, 2016, the institution's name was changed once again, this time to Tennessee Wesleyan University.

The productions of the Theatre Department are held at theaters across campus, such as the Patricelli '92 Theatre and the Thad Smotherman Theatre. According to Dean of Freshmen Joe Brown, the theater in the Fine Arts Building is haunted by a ghost named Georgia, who has been sighted in one of the seats in the auditorium. The theater in Townsend Hall also has a haunted reputation. Actors, directors and stage crews have heard phantom footsteps backstage. Occasionally, rehearsals have been interrupted by mysterious crashing sounds whose source was never found. Students have christened the ghost Sylvia because of a piece of graffiti written on one of the backstage walls: "Sylvia was here." After the final rehearsal for a production of *The Crucible*, the director was congratulating the cast for a job well done when all at once, the work lights were turned off. At that time, the only way to turn off the lights was to unplug them. The director was walking backstage to plug the cord back in when the lights came back on. Instead of being irked by the spirit's annoying interruption, the director preferred to focus on the ghost's contribution to the building's energy.

Tennessee Wesleyan College started out as Athens Female College in 1857. *Wikimedia Commons.*

The Methodist Conference Center, students say, is haunted by the ghost of Audrey Dillow. She was a graduate of Tennessee Wesleyan University who donated her house to her alma mater shortly before her death. A number of staff members who work in the building have sensed her presence keeping track of their movements through the house. One female employee heard the creaking sound of Dillow's rocking chair rocking in Dillow's bedroom.

UNIVERSITY OF TENNESSEE

Knoxville

The University of Tennessee was originally founded as Blount College in 1794, two years before Tennessee became a state. It was originally founded on Gay Street in Knoxville. This all-male school was rechartered as East Tennessee College in 1806. In order to have room to spread out, Thomas Jefferson recommended that the school move a larger site in town. In 1826, it was relocated to "the Hill," which became a main feature of the campus. During the Civil War, Fort Boyington was built on the Hill across from a large entrenchment called Fort Sanders. On November 19, 1863, eight hundred Confederate soldiers were lost in a charge up the hill to Fort Sanders. The university reopened after the Civil War. While the school was being rebuilt, it was designated as a land grant university by the state legislature. In 1879, the school was renamed the University of Tennessee. It participated in the V-12 Navy College Training Program during World War II. Today, the University of Tennessee is the flagship of the University of Tennessee statewide system and is regarded as one of the top ten universities in the entire country.

The long history of the University of Tennessee reasserts itself in the school's ghost stories. The Hill is a large green space where students have heard the howling of a large, wolflike creature called a barghest. In an article appearing in the *UT Daily Beacon*, Alexandra DeMarco theorized that, based on eyewitnesses' description of the beast, it could actually be a large, pantherine creature called a Wampus Cat. According to Cherokee folklore, a young woman dressed in a mountain lion skin was transformed into a phantom feline, the Wampus Cat, after spying on a forbidden ritual.

In the same article, DeMarco writes about the ghost of a young man wearing a bowler hat and a celluloid collar who has also been seen walking on the Hill with his head down. Supposedly, he is the ghost of a young man who killed himself in the 1930s after being jilted by his girlfriend. He seems to be perfectly normal until he tips his hat at young ladies, revealing a large bullet hole in his head.

Many colleges and universities have haunted libraries, and the University of Tennessee is no exception. The Hoskins Library was built in 1931 and renovated in the 1950s. It is said to be haunted by a female spirit known only as Evening Primrose. She announces her presence with the fragrant smell of just-baked cornbread. She also pushes books off the shelves and rides the elevator. No one knows her true identity.

Strong Hall, a woman's dormitory, was built in 1925. It was named after Sophronia Strong. Born in 1817, she married a Knoxville physician named Joseph C. Strong in 1833. Following her death, her son, Benjamin Strong, made a sizable contribution to the university for the construction of a woman's residence hall with a wildflower garden in the courtyard. Apparently, she liked the building that bears her name so much that she has taken up residence there herself. Students say she is a mischievous spirit who locks students out of their rooms. Some say that she takes the form of a ball of light, floating around the hallways. Supposedly, two young women who were fighting in one of rooms stopped abruptly when they noticed the figure of a stern woman staring them with her hands on her hips.

Blount Hall was built in 1900. When it was razed in 1979, workers discovered the bones of eight Union soldiers in shallow graves. Their remains were interred in the National Cemetery. The spirits of the soldiers, which have been sighted walking around the Blount Hall corridors, make regular appearances near Perkins Hall, where students have seen them perusing maps of the university.

According to folklore, constructing a house or building on top of an Indian burial ground is never a good idea. Three buildings on campus—McClung

Museum, Reese Hall and the Agriculture Campus—are believed to have been built on top of an unknown number of Native American burial sites. Not surprisingly, a high amount of paranormal activity has been reported in all of these buildings. Students walking through Reese Hall have had encounters with dark entities known as "shadow people."

BIBLIOGRAPHY

Books

Asfar, Dan, and Edrick Thay. *Ghost Stories of the Civil War*. Auburn, WA: Ghost House Books, 2003.

Bell, Charles Bailey. *The Bell Witch of Tennessee*. Nashville, TN: Charles Elder—Bookseller, 1934.

Brown, Alan. *Haunted Tennessee*. Mechanicsburg, PA: Stackpole Press, 2009.

Bush, Bryan, and Thomas Freese. *Haunted Battlefields of the South*. Atglen, PA: Shiffer, 2010.

Coleman, Christopher K. *Ghosts and Haunts of Tennessee*. Winston-Salem, NC: John F. Blair, 2011.

Cunningham, Laura. *Haunted Memphis*. Charleston, SC: The History Press, 2009.

Hillhouse, Larry. *Ghosts of Lookout Mountain*. Wever, IA: Quixote Press, 2010.

Jameson, W.C. *Buried Treasures of the Appalachians*. Atlanta, GA: August House, 1991.

Judson, Katharine Berry. *Myths and Legends of the Great Plains*. Chicago: A.C. McClurg, 1913.

Kennedy, Frances H., ed. *The Civil War Battlefield Guide*. Boston: Houghton Mifflin, 1990.

Kotarski, Georgiana C. *Ghosts of the Southern Tennessee Valley*. Winston-Salem, NC: John F. Blair, 2006.

Martin, LeRoy A. *A History of Tennessee Wesleyan College*. Self-published, 1957.

Mott, A.S. *Ghost Stories of Tennessee*. Auburn, WA: Lone Pine, 2005.

Penoit, Jessica, and Amy Petulla. *Haunted Chattanooga*. Charleston, SC: The History Press, 2011.

Price, Charles Edwin. *More Haunted Tennessee*. Jonesboro, TN: Overmountain Press, 1999

Russell, Randy, and Janet Barnett. *The Granny Curse and Other Ghosts and Legends from East Tennessee*. Durham, NC: Blair Press, 1999.

Taylor, Troy. *Season of the Witch*. Alton, IL: White Chapel Press, 1999.

———. *Spirits of the Civil War*. Alton, IL: Whitechapel Press, 1999.

Twain, Mark. *Life on the Mississippi*. New York: Bantam, 1981.

Van West, Carroll, ed. *Tennessee History: The Land, The People, and the Culture*. Knoxville: University of Tennessee Press, 1998.

Windham, Kathryn Tucker. *13 Tennessee Ghosts and Jeffrey*. Tuscaloosa: University of Alabama Press, 1977.

Internet Articles

Ackerson, Leslie. “Friday the 13th Ghosts, Duels, & Falling Glass Fill 200 Years of Haunted History at Bijou Theatre.” WBIR 10, last updated September 13, 2019. https://www.wbir.com/article/news/local/51-608699714.

Adventure Anderson County. “Haunted Places in East Tennessee.” https://www.adventureanderson.com/blog/haunted-places-in-east-tennessee.

Alcatraz History. “George ‘Machine Gun” Kelly.” https://www.alcatrazhistory.com/mgk.htm.

Alexander, Nicole. “Spooky MTSU: Campus Ghost Stories.” Middle Tennessee State University, October 29, 2021. https://mtsunews.com/spooky-mtsu-campus-ghost-stories/.

Allen, Chuck. “Kid Curry Takes on the Knoxville Police Department, Part 1.” Knoxify, June 11, 2009. https://knoxify.com/kid-curry-takes-on-the-knoxville-police-department-part-1/.

———. “Kid Curry Takes on the Knoxville Police Department, Part 2.” Knoxify, July 15, 2009. https://knoxify.com/kid-curry-takes-on-the-knoxville-police-department-part-2/.

Allison, Autumn. “APSU Ghost Stories Feature Mule, Civil War.” Leaf Chronicle. https://www.theleafchronicle.com/story/

news/local/2016/10/28/apsu-ghost-stories-feature-mule-civil-war/92698256/.

———. "Ghost of 'Margaret' Said to Haunt APSU's Trahern Building." Leaf Chronicle. https://theleafchronicle.com/story/news/local/2016/10/28/trahern-ghost-stories-have-ties-apsu-history/92697730/.

All Things Cruise. "Historic *Delta Queen*'s Resident Ghost." https://allthingscruise.com/historic-delta-queens-resident-ghost/.

Andrew Jackson's Hermitage. "The Hermitage Mansion Story." https://thehermitage/com/learn/mansion-grounds/mansion-story/.

Appalachia Bare. "'A Strange and Frightful Being'—Appalachia's Folklore Creatures Part 3." https://www.appalachiabare.com/a-strange-and-frightful-being-appalachias-folklore-creatures-part-3/.

Auto Simple. "5 Haunted Roads & Places in Tennessee." October 26, 2017. https://www.autosimple.com/blog/5-haunted-roads-places-tennessee/.

Biography.com. "Machine Gun Kelly." https://www.biography.com/crime-figure/machine-gun-kelly.

Blue Ridge—Smoky Mtn Highlander. "Cherokee Myths & Legends of the Black Bear." https://theblueridgehighlander.com/Cherokee-Legends-of-the-Black-Bear.php.

Broome, Fiona. "'Pig Man Ghosts'—Real or Urban Legend?" Hollow Hill. hollowhill.com/pigman-ghosts/.

Brownlee, Karen. "What It's Like to Work at the Most Haunted Bar in America." Vice, December 9, 2017. https://www.vice.com/en/article/vvxnmb/this-is-what-its-like-to-work-at-the-most-haunted-bar-in-america.

Burdine, Nikki. "Spirits of Children, Soldiers Still Visit Lotz House in Franklin." WKRN.com, October 30, 2019. https://www.wkrn.com/special-reports/haunted-tennessee/spirits-of-children-soldiers-still-visit-lotz-house-in-franklin/.

CabinsUSA. "10 Haunted Places in the Smoky Mountains." https://www.cabinsusa.com/smoky-mountains-blog/post/17/10-haunted-places-in-the-smoky-mountains.php.

Clements, Miranda R. "Read House Hotel." Tennessee Encyclopedia, last updated March 1, 2018. https://tennesseeencyclopedia.net/entries/read-house-hotel/.

Coleman, Christopher. *The Late Unpleasantness: A Civil War Blog*. https://thelateunpleasantness.wordpress.com.

Cryptid Wiki. "Tennessee Wildman." https://cryptidz.fandom.com/wiki/Tennessee_Wildman.

Darknite125. "Creepy Mysteries: Ghosts of Earnestine's and Hazel's." Funk's House of Geekery, December 24, 2020. https://houseofgeekery.com/2020/12/24/creepy-mysteries-ghosts-of-earnestine-and-hazels/.

Dark Tales. "The Disappearance of Dennis Martin." June 4, 2020. https://darktales.blog/2020/06/04/the-disappearance-of-dennis-martin/.

Day, Katie. "ETSU Is One of the Most Haunted Campuses in the Nation." *East Tennessean*, October 29, 2018. https://easttennessean.com/2018/10/29/etsu-is-one-of-the-most-haunted-campuses-in-the-nation/.

Dickson Post. "'White Bluff Screamer' Tops Local Story List." https://www.dicksonpost.com/townnews/zoology/white-bluff-screamer-tops-local-story.list/article_c93a0db2-3366-11ec-8853-ffd08131840b.html.

Egnatz, Erin. "Haunted Stones River National Battlefield." Horror. https://vocal.media/horror/haunted-stones-river-national-battlefield.

Falcon Rest Mansion & Gardens. https://falconrest.com/.

Fox, Randy. "The Great UFO Wave of 1973 Brought an 'Autumn of Aliens' to Middle Tennessee." Nashville Scene, October 31, 2013. https://www.nashvillescene.com/news/the-great-ufo-wave-of-1973-brought-an-autumn-of-aliens-to-middle-tennessee/article_1aedcb58-7b62-512d-9dc1-77bebdecb87a.html.

Geocaching. "The Lost Shults Mine." https://www.geocaching.com/geocache/GCJH6N_the-lost-shultsmine?guid=607f8dad-7e5.

Ghost City Tours. "The Ghosts of the Haunted Read House Hotel." https://ghostcitytours.com/chattanooga/haunted-chattanooga/read-house-hotel/.

———. "The Ghosts of the Haunted Ryman Auditorium." https://ghostcitytours.com/nashville/haunted-nashville/ryman-auditorium-ghosts/.

———. "The Ghosts of the Nashville City Cemetery." https://ghostcitytours.com/nashville/haunted-nashville/nashville-city-cemetery/.

———. "The Ghosts of Union Station Hotel." https://ghostcitytours.com/nashville/haunted-nashville/haunted-union-hotel/.

———. "Nashville's Haunted Hermitage." https://ghostcitytours.com/nashville/haunted-nashville/ghosts-hermitage/.

Greenbrier Campground Great Smoky Mountains. "The Legend of Perry Shults and the Lost Smoky Mountain Gold Mine in Greenbrier." July 31, 2016. https://www.smokymountaincamping.com/blog/legend-of-the-lost-smoky-mountain-gold.

Guillon, John. "Is Gatlinburg Haunted? 6 Best Ghost Stories of the Smoky Mountains." TheSmokies.com, last updated September 14, 2022. https://www.thesmokies.com/haunted-smoky-mountains/.

Haunted Houses. "Carnton Mansion." hauntedhouses.com/Tennessee/carnton-mansion/.

———. "Orpheum Theatre." hauntedhouses.com/tennessee/Orpheum-theatre/.

HearthSide Cabin Rentals in the Smokies. "3 Smoky Mountain Ghost Stories That Will Scare Your Socks Off." August 30, 2018. https://www.hearthsidecabinrentals.com/blog/smoky-mountains/smoky-mountain-ghost-stories/.

Hill, Paige. "Visitors Aren't Allowed Upstairs at Loretta Lynn Ranch for a Reason." WKRN.com, October 29, 2019. https://www.wkrn.com/special-reports/haunted-tennessee/visitors-arent-allowed-upstairs-at-loretta-lynn-ranch-for-a-reason/.

Historic Memphis. "Historic Woodruff-Fontaine House…Famous Old Memphis Home." https://historic-memphis.com/memphis-historic/woodruff-fontaine/woodruff-fontaine.html.

Historynet. "Ex-Rebel Cullen Baker Was a Post-War Murdering Madman." https://www.historynet.com/how-tennessee-born-killer-cullen-baker-hit-his-stride-after-the-civil-war/.

The History Junkie. "Cullen Baker—One of the West's First Bad Men." https://thehistoryjunkie.com/cullen-baker-one-of-the-wests-first-bad-men/.

———. "Robert Clay Allison Biography." https://thehistoryjunkie.com/robert-clay-allison-biography/.

History.com. "Battle of Fort Donelson." https://www.history.com/topics/american-civil-war/battle-of-fort-donelson.

———. "Battle of Lookout Mountain." http://history.com/this-day-in-history/battle-of-lookout-mountain.

Jayz Ghost Stories from the Eastern United States. "Ghosts of ETSU." https://jayboy74.tripod.com/story14.html.

Jim. "Classic Mystery Legend: The Disappearance of David Lang." Unexplainable.net, February 24, 2008. https://www.unexplainable.net/mysteries/classic-mystery-legend-the-disappearance-of-david-lang.php.

Katie-Beth. "Get Spooked by History and Haunts at the Hermitage." *Her Life in Ruins* (blog). https://herlifeinruins.com/haunts-at-the-hermitage/.

KingsportTN.gov. "Sensabaugh Tunnel." https://www.kingsporttn.gov/sensabaugh-tunnel/.

Lakin, Matt. "Archive: Notorious Outlaw, Notable Invention among Biggest Stories for Sentinel in New Century." Knox News. https://www.knoxnews.com/story/news/local/2018/06/26/notorious-outlaw-notable-invention-among-biggest-stories-senteinel-new-century/735481002/.

Legends of America. "Cades Cove Scenic Loop, Tennessee." https://www.lendsofamerica.com/cades-cove-scenic-loop/.

———. "Harvey Logan, aka "Kid Curry"—The Wildest of the Wild Bunch." https://www.legendsofamerica.com/we-harveylogan/.

Leonard, Austin. "The Cryptids of Tennessee." *Kayseean*, October 19, 2021. https://thekayseean.com/life-and-culture/the-cryptids-of-tennessee/.

Lester, Dee Gee. "Hunt-Phelan House." Tennessee Encyclopedia, last updated March 1, 2018. https://tennesseeencyclopedia.net/entries/hunt-phelan-house/.

Lynch, Michael. "Communication and a Cryptid on the Tennessee Frontier." *Past in the Present* (blog), February 11, 2017. https://pastinthepresent.wordpress.com/2017/02/11/communication-and-a-cryptid-on-the-tennessee-frontier/.

McGee, Nikki. "Mysterious Disappearance of Murfreesboro Woman Haunts Prosecutor More Than a Decade Later." WKRN.com, last updated December 21, 2020. https://www.wkrn.com/unsolved-tennessee/mysterious-disappearance-of-murfreesboro-woman-haunts-prosecutor-more-than-a-decade-later/.

Memphis Heritage Inc. "The Hunt-Phelan House." https://www.memphisheritage.org/hunt-phelan-house/.

Middle Tennessee State University. "A Brief History of MTSU." https://mtsu.edu/about/history.php.

Millington, TN Memories and News. "The Thrill of Pig Man Bridge." https://facebook.com/MillingtonTNMemories/posts/the-thrill-of-pig-man-bridgeif-you-were-much-like-myself-as-a-teenager-there-wer1584-7738703664/.

Mississippi Encyclopedia. "John Murrell." https://mississippiencyclopedia.org/entries/john-murrell/.

Morley, Gabriel. "A Librarian's Voyage into the Paranormal." Tennessee Library Association. https://www.tnla.org/page/477.

My Smoky Mountain Guide. "A Brief History of Cades Cove." https://mysmokymountainguide.com/gsmnp/brief-history-cades-cove/.

Nashville Ghosts. "Blood Soaked Land: Haunted Wheatlands." https://nashvilleghosts.com/haunted-wheatlands-plantation/.

———.“Haunted Carnton Plantation.” https://nashvilleghosts.com/haunted-carnton-plantation/.

———.“Haunted Nashville City Cemetery.” https://nashvilleghosts.com/nashville-city-cemetery/.

———. “The Hermitage.” https://nashvilleghosts.com/the-hermitage/.

———. “Loretta Lynn Ranch.” https://nashvilleghosts.com/loretta-lynn-ranch/.

———. “Union Station Hotel.” https://nashvilleghosts.com/union-station-hotel/.

National Park Service. “Dover Hotel (Surrender House).” https://www.nps.gov/fodo/learn/photosmultimedia/tourstop10.htm.

———. “Fort Donelson National Cemetery.” https://www.nps.gov/fodo/planyourvisit/fortdonelsonnationalcemetery.htm.

Netemeyer, Sarah. “Loretta Lynn’s Hurricane Mills Property Is a Real Haunted House.” Countryfancast, October 8, 2020. https://countryfancast.com/loretta-lynn-hurricane-mills/.

Nemarich, Kate. “Haunted Tri-Cities: A Look Inside the Halls of ETSU.” WJHL.com, last updated November 4, 2021. https://www.wjhl.com/haunted-tri-cities/haunted-tri-cities-a-look-inside-the-halls-of-etsu/.

NOOGAtoday. “Ruby Falls Deemed an Official Haunted Location.” https://noogatoday.6amcity.com.

Orpheum Theatre Group. “History of the Orpheum Theatre.” https://orpheum-memphis.com/about-us/history/.

Palazzo, Julia. “Soldiers and Spirits Haunt Stones River Battlefield in Murfreesboro.” WKRN.com, Octoeber 29, 2020. https://www.wkrn.com/special-reports/haunted-tennessee/soldiers-and-spirits-haunt-stones-river-battlefield-in-murfreesboro/.

Phillips, Betsy. “The Legend of Disappearing David Lang.” Nashville Scene, May 29, 2014. https://www.nashvillescene.com/news/pithinthewind/the-legend-of-disappearing-david-lang/article_f47328b7-2db2-53d0-b8be-2e3604969aa6.html.

Piddlin. “Spearfinger—A Legend of the Cherokee.” Last updated November 17, 2020. https://piddlin.com/library/smoky-mountains/spearfinger.

PigeonForge.com. “Spooky Smokies: Haunted Places and Smoky Mountain Legends.” October 6, 2020. https://www.pigeonforge.com/smoky-mountain-legends.

Pitsiladis, D.J. “Nightmare Fuel: The White Bluff Screamer.” Horror Addicts, June 7, 2021. https://horroraddicts.wordpress.com/2021/06/07/nightmare-fuel-the-white-bluff-screamer/.

The Place of Scary—Haunted Places. "Fort Donelson National Battlefield/Cemetery—Dover, Tennessee." https://hauntedplacesofusa.blogspot.com/2009/10/fort-donelson-national-battlefield.html.

Powell, Lewis O., IV. "Certified Haunted in Tennessee–Chattanooga." *Southern Spirit Guide* (blog), September 30, 2014. https://www.southernspiritguide.org/certified-haunted-in-tennessee-newsworthy-haunts/.

———. "Haunted Tennessee, Briefly Noted." *Southern Spirit Guide* (blog), January 26, 2018. https://www.southernspiritguide.org/haunted-tennessee-briefly-noted/.

———. "'A Multitude of the Heavenly Host'—Old Gray Cemetery." *Southern Spirit Guide* (blog), September 24, 2012. https://www.southernspiritguide.org/a-multitude-of-the-heavenly-host-old-gray-cemetery-photos/.

Quimby's Cruising Guide. "Ghost Hunting on the *Delta Queen*." October 21, 2013. https://quimbyscruisingguide.com/ghost-hunting-on-the-delta-queen/.

RareGoldNuggets.com. "John Murrell's Lost Treasure." October 2, 2017. https://raregoldnuggets.com/?p=5261.

RedNation. "How the Black Bear Lost His Tail." February 23, 2014. rednation.org/index.php?topic=35/0.

Reelfoot Outdoors. "The Legend of Chief Reelfoot." https://www.reelfoot.com/legend_1.htm.

Roadtrippers. "A Bittersweet Road Trip: The Trail of Tears to Lovers Leap." https://maps.roadtrippers.com/trips/18891781.

———. "The Hauntings of Red Ash." https://maps.roadtrippers.com/us/caryville-tn/points-of-interest/the-hauntings-of-red-ash.

Robertson, Rickey. "The Robber John Murrell and His Famous Hideouts." Stephen F. Austin State University, November 2012. https://www.sfasu.edu/heritagecenter/5818.asp.

Ryman. "Explore the Ryman Timeline." https://ryman.com/history/.

Tabler, Dave. "The (Accidental) Discovery of a Lifetime." Appalachian History. https://www.appalachianhistory.net/2018/07/accidental-discovery-of-lifetime.html.

Smith, Jen. "History of Cades Cove." National Park Service. https://www.nps.gov/grsm/learn/historyculture/cades-cove-history.htm.

Smith, Lindi. "The Strange Story of Loretta Lynn's Haunted Hurricane Mills Mansion." Wide Open Country, October 30, 2021. https://www.

wideopencountry.com/story-behind-loretta-lynns-haunted-hurricane-mills-plantation/.

Sonnichsen, C.L. "Allison, Robert Clay (1841–1887)." Texas State Historical Association, first published 1952, last updated November 1, 1994. https://www.tshaonline.org/handbook/entries/allison-robert-clay.

Southern Ghost Stories. "Tennessee Ghost Stories: The Hunt-Phelan House." southernghoststories.com/Tennessee-ghost-stories-the-hunt-phelan-house.

Spivak, Lexi. "Gatlinburg Restaurant Haunted by Ghost Bride, Others." WATE 6, October 28, 2021. https://www.wate.com/news/as-seen-on-wate/haunted-tennessee/gatlinburg-restaurant-haunted-by-ghost-bride-others.

Stockton, Steve. "Ghost of the Suicide Bride." Horror. https://vocal.media/horror/ghost-of-the-suicide-bride.

Tennessee Haunted Houses. "Experience the Legend of Halloween's Tall Betsy!" October 30, 2018. https://www.tennesseehauntedhouses.com/blog/halloween-legend-tall-betsy.html.

———. "Lincoln Memorial University—Grant Lee Hall—Harrogate TN Haunted Place." https://www.tennesseehauntedhouses.com/real-haunt/lincoln-memorial-university--grant-lee-hall.html.

Tennessee Myths and Legends. "Bell Witch." https://sharetngov.tnsosfiles.com/tsla/exhibits/myth/bellwitch.htm.

———. "Meriwether Lewis National Monument." https://sharetngov.tnsosfiles.com/tsla/exhibits/myth/ghosts.htm.

Tennessee Wesleyan College Merner Pfeiffer Library. "The Legend of Nocatula." October 10, 2007. https://twcbookwise.wordpress.com/2007/10/10/the-legend-of-nocatula/.

Texas Cryptid Hunter. "What Happened to Dennis Martin?" July 4, 2020. http://texascryptidhunter.blogspot.com/2020/07/what-happened-to-dennis-martin.html.

TreasureNet. "Bradley County Tenn Lost Confederate Payroll." https://www.treasurenet.com/threads/bradley-county-tenn-lost-confederate-payroll.155765/.

Tripadvisor. "Beautifully Haunting: Review of Fort Donelson National Battlefield." https://www.tripadvisor.com/ShowUserRivews-g60808-d143130-r3566844-Fort_Donelson_National_Battlefield-Dover_Tennessee.html.

Tucker, Lori. "Knoxville's Notable Past Marked in the Old Gray Cemetery." WATE 6, October 28, 2020. https://www.wate.com/news/

as-seen-on-wate/haunted-tennessee/knoxvilles-notable-past-marked-in-the-old-gray-cemetery/.

The University of Tennessee Knoxville News. "Five Haunted Spots at UT." October 31, 2016. https://news.utk.edu/2016/10/31/haunted-spots-ut/.

Violet Sky. "The Hauntings of the Lotz House." *Violet Sky Adventures* (blog). https://violetskyadventures.com/the-hauntings-of-the-lotz-house/.

Visit My Smokies. "5 Common Great Smoky Mountain Myths and Legends." June 14, 2019. https://www.visitmysmokies.com/blog/smoky-mountains/great-smoky-mountain-myths-legends/.

War, Samantha. "The 6 Most Haunted Places in Tennessee." Budget Travel, October 19, 2020. https://www.budgettravel.com/article/five-haunted-places-in-Tennessee.

Watts, Kyle. "Graduate Student Explores the 'Ghost Stories of Austin Peay.'" Austin Peay State University, October 30, 2019. https://www.apsu.edu/news/october-2019-ghost-stories.php.

West, Mike. "Headless Horseman Haunts Stones River Battlefield." *Murfreesboro Post*, October 18, 2009. https://www.murfreesboropost.com/community/headless-horseman-haunts-stones-river-battlefield/article_e95f619b-fdc2-505a-8f2a-c8b1da56b6d7.html.

Williams, Frank B., Jr. "East Tennessee State University." Tennessee Encyclopedia, last updated March 1, 2018. https://tennesseeencyclopedia.net/entries/east-tennessee-state-university/.

Williamson Source. "4 Real-Life Haunted Places in Franklin." October 29, 2016. https://williamsonsource.com/4-real-life-haunted-places-in-franklin-third-ave/.

World History. "Wild Bunch—Capturing a Train Robber: Kid Curry's Escapades in Knoxville Tennessee." May 21, 2017. https://worldhistory.us/american-history/this-wild-wild-west/wild-bunch-capturing-a-train-robber-kid-currys-escapades-in-knoxville-tennessee.php.

Newspaper, Magazine and Journal Articles

Balloch, Jim. "From the Archives: Search in Smokies for Lost Boy, Dennis Martin, Produces Lessons for Future Searches." *Knoxville News Sentinel*, October 2, 2018.

Bartlett, Kerri. "Lotz House Unexplained Phenomena Draws Travel Channel's 'Haunted Live.'" *Williamson Herald*, October 5, 2018.

DeMarco, Alexandra. "The Most Haunted Spots around UT's Campus." *UT Daily Beacon*, October 30, 2019.

Erickson, Wallace, Gregory D. John and David P. Young Jr. *A Summary and Comparison of Bird Mortality from Anthropogenic Causes with an Emphasis on Collisions*. USDA, Forest Service Gen. Tech. Rep. PSW-GTR-191.2005.

Finger, Michael. "The Real Story of Machine Gun Kelly." *Memphis Magazine*, July 10, 2017.

Floyd, E. Randall. "The Flintville Monster, Tennessee 1997." *Augusta Georgia Chronicle*, April 6, 1997.

Lauderdale, Vance. "When Snakes Rained on Memphis." *Memphis: The City Magazine*, June 27, 2019.

Shubauer, Liz. "Who Haunts the Lotz House? What to Know about Site of Civil War Battle." *The Tennessean*, October 5, 2018.

Watts, Micaela A., and Jennifer Chandler. "Bones Discovered in the Walls at Earnestine and Hazel's during Restoration Work." *Commercial Appeal*, July 18, 2019.

Whittle, Dan. "Ghost Rider Haunts Battlefield." *Cannon Courier*, October 22, 2013.

Willard, Michelle. "Was Marcie Smith Killed by Her Husband?" *Memphis Voice*, June 18, 2018.

ABOUT THE AUTHOR

Alan Brown teaches English at the University of West Alabama in Livingston, Alabama. Alan has written primarily about southern ghost lore, a passion that has taken him to haunted places throughout the entire Deep South, as well as parts of the Midwest and the Southwest. Alan's wife, Marilyn, accompanies him on these trips and occasionally serves as his "ghost magnet." Her encounters with the spirit world have been incorporated into a number of Alan's books.